Global Trends in Museum Diplomacy

Global Trends in Museum Diplomacy traces the transformation of museums from publicly or privately funded heritage institutions into active players in the economic sector of culture. Exploring how this transformation reconfigured cultural diplomacy, the book argues that museums have become autonomous diplomatic players on the world stage.

The book offers a comparative analysis across a range of case studies in order to demonstrate that museums have gone global in the era of neo-liberal globalisation. Grincheva focuses first on the Solomon R. Guggenheim Foundation, which is well known for its bold revolutionising strategies of global expansion: museum franchising and global corporatisation. The book then goes on to explore how these strategies were adopted across museums around the world and analyses two cases of post-Guggenheim developments in China and Russia: the K11 Art Mall in Hong Kong and the International Network of Foundations of the State Hermitage Museum in Russia. These cases from more authoritarian political regimes evidence the emergence of alternative avenues of museum diplomacy that no longer depend on government commissions to serve immediate geopolitical interests.

Global Trends in Museum Diplomacy will be a valuable resource for students, scholars and practitioners of contemporary museology and cultural diplomacy. Documenting new developments in museum diplomacy, the book will be particularly interesting to museum and heritage practitioners and policymakers involved in international exchanges or official programs of cultural diplomacy.

Natalia Grincheva is a Research Fellow in the Research Unit of Public Cultures at the University of Melbourne. She is also Lead CI and Conceptual Designer of the award-winning digital mapping system Museum Soft Power Map. Dr Grincheva has been awarded numerous academic awards and fellowships, including Fulbright (2007–2009), Quebec Fund (2011–2013), Australian Endeavour (2012–2013), SOROS (2013–2014) and others. She has successfully implemented a number of research projects on new forms of contemporary diplomacy developed by the largest internationally recognised museums in North America, Europe and Asia–Pacific.

Museums in Focus

Series Editor: Kylie Message

Committed to the articulation of big, even risky, ideas in small format publications, 'Museums in Focus' challenges authors and readers to experiment with, innovate, and press museums and the intellectual frameworks through which we view these. It offers a platform for approaches that radically rethink the relationships between cultural and intellectual dissent and crisis and debates about museums, politics and the broader public sphere.

'Museums in Focus' is motivated by the intellectual hypothesis that museums are not innately 'useful', safe' or even 'public' places, and that recalibrating our thinking about them might benefit from adopting a more radical and oppositional form of logic and approach. Examining this problem requires a level of comfort with (or at least tolerance of) ideas of crisis, dissent, protest and radical thinking, and authors might benefit from considering how cultural and intellectual crisis, regeneration and anxiety have been dealt with in other disciplines and contexts.

Interpreting Objects in the Hybrid Museum
Collections and Cultural Policy
Helena Robinson

Museums and Racism
Kylie Message

https://www.routledge.com/Museums-in-Focus/book-series/MIF

MUSEUMS IN FOCUS

Logo by James Verdon (2017)

Global Trends in Museum Diplomacy

Post-Guggenheim Developments

Natalia Grincheva

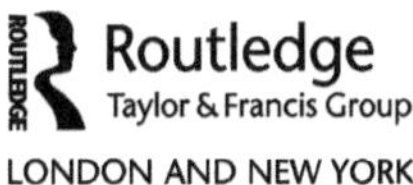

LONDON AND NEW YORK

First published 2020
by Routledge
2 Park Square, Milton Park, Abingdon, Oxon OX14 4RN

and by Routledge
605 Third Avenue, New York, NY 10017

First issued in paperback 2021

Routledge is an imprint of the Taylor & Francis Group, an informa business

British Library Cataloguing-in-Publication Data
A catalogue record for this book is available from the British Library

Library of Congress Cataloging-in-Publication Data
A catalog record for this book has been requested

ISBN 13: 978-0-367-78794-3 (pbk)
ISBN 13: 978-0-8153-7094-9 (hbk)

Typeset in Times New Roman
by Apex CoVantage, LLC

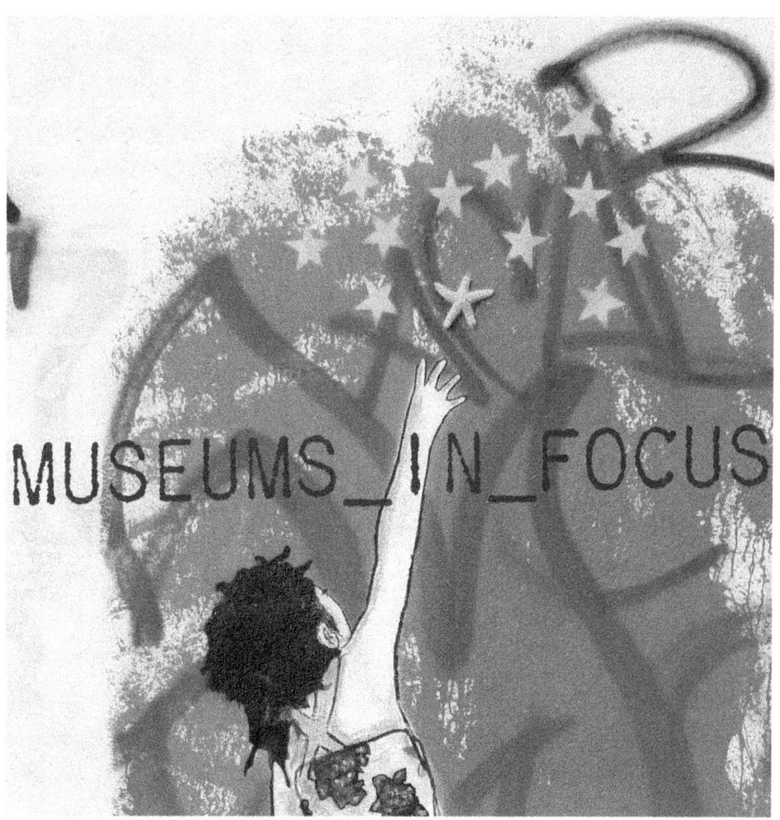

Anonymous graffiti, Athens. Image and logo by James Verdon (2017).

Contents

Figures

Introduction

Museum diplomacy then and now

This book brings together two important topics that have not been explored in correlation with each other either in academia or in the professional world of museums. First, it focuses on a significant transformation of museums in the twenty-first century. In an era of increasing globalisation, museums have grown from publicly or privately funded repositories of cultural heritage into active players in the economic sector of culture. Second, the book traces how this transformation has challenged, advanced and reconfigured cultural diplomacy. It argues that contemporary museums have gone global and become key diplomatic players on the world stage without traditional patronage or support from their national governments.

Cultural diplomacy has traditionally been a strategic instrument of national governments to achieve foreign policy objectives. Though defined as an "exchange of ideas, information, art and other aspects of culture between countries to improve mutual understanding" (Cummings 2003, 1), it has always been a tool to communicate to the outside world. Nation states have employed cultural diplomacy to facilitate cross-cultural events or a series of cultural activities among different countries to achieve political or economic goals in the international arena.

Different states have supported the international missions of museums to promote national cultural ideas and values abroad to pursue strategic geopolitical interests. Museums have engaged in diplomatic activities through exporting individual collections of art since the Renaissance (Arndt 2005; Digout 2006; Sylvester 2009). For example, since its founding, the British Museum in London has been an important actor in cultural diplomacy, following its mandate as set by parliamentarians in 1753: "To allow visitors to address through objects, both ancient and more recent, questions of contemporary politics and international relations" (MacGregor 2004, 2).

A classic example of museum diplomacy is a series of large-scale exports of abstract expressionism in the epoch of the Cold War. During this period, American museums served as cultural ambassadors to other parts of the world to fight against communism (de Hart Mathews 1976; Hobbs 1997;

Ninkovich 1997). Following the end of World War II, hundreds of exhibitions of American modern paintings sponsored by the United States (U.S.) government travelled to Europe, Latin America, Asia, Africa and eventually Soviet Russia. For example, the Museum of Modern Art was directly funded by the government to organise large and expensive exhibits, such as "The Modern Art in the US" (1956) and "The New American Painting" (1958), in Western Bloc European countries through the Congress for Cultural Freedom program (Cockcroft 1985).

These cases of cultural diplomacy demonstrate the powerful role of government in setting cultural agendas, defining geopolitical focus and commissioning the international activities of museums. Embarking on international partnerships with overseas counterparts, museums have depended on government support and served as political agents for promoting national ideologies and cultural values abroad (Arndt 2005). In recent decades, though, museums – as dynamic institutions reflecting the economic and political changes of neo-liberal globalisation – have changed dramatically. Challenged by gradually decreasing government funding, museums in different countries around the world have developed new ways to sustain their expensive operations in not only the national but also the international context (Alexander 1999; Fraser 2006; Grincheva 2016, 2017). The next section provides illustrations of this phenomenon across museums and countries.

The protagonists of the global expansion, the protagonists of the book

The Solomon R. Guggenheim Foundation is a world-recognised museum of contemporary and modern art, but it is also rather well known for revolutionising the professional world of museums with two key strategies of global expansion. These strategies are *museum franchising* and *global corporatisation. Museum franchising* is a hybrid form of museum management. It is a combination of non-profit organisational management and a new behaviour that sees museums as more autonomous actors in creative economy. Like in the business world, museum franchising is a contract-based practice of granting the right to use a brand name and employ a unique operational model in different places across countries (Dicke 1992). However, in contrast to business practices, museum franchising helps to advance the organisational mission rather than to merely maximise economic return.

With a main museum in New York (1939) and branches in Venice (1951), Bilbao (1997), Berlin (1997–2013), Las Vegas (2001–2008) and a planned franchise in Abu Dhabi, the Guggenheim has developed a strong infrastructure to support its international programming. This network expanded the Guggenheim's exhibition spaces across borders, reaching much wider and more diverse audiences on a global scale. Having branches across countries allows the museum to circulate its collections and exhibitions, develop its global brand name and, as a result, attract multimillion-dollar sponsorship opportunities.

This corporate sponsorship, though, is only a part of the global corporatisation strategy, successfully trialled by Guggenheim. *Global corporatisation*, as a practice adopted in the museum world, draws on the commercialisation of museum activities. It can include shopping, dining and other leisure or entertainment opportunities that bring more diverse customers to the door. In many cases, this practice is determined by reinforced corporate museum governance, and by partnerships with transnational corporations that usually seek to draw on a museum brand to win new markets. The Guggenheim's global programs, for example, include various projects generously supported by "image-conscious foreign corporations" such as Hugo Boss, UBS Wealth Management, Delta Airlines and Google, to name a few.

The famous BMW Guggenheim Lab, sustained by the iconic German car brand, toured around the world from New York to Berlin to Mumbai. Another well-known example is a series of blockbuster exhibitions on Giorgio Armani. The first-ever exhibit on fashion in an art museum travelled widely across the globe, from Las Vegas to Tokyo. Global corporatisation strategies did more than make Guggenheim more sustainable and competitive in the global economic sector of culture. They allowed it to implement large-scale international projects across continents. Drawing on a transnational network of corporate connections, Guggenheim was able to expand its reach and presence far beyond North America and Europe. Its new curatorial residencies, collection acquisition projects and audience development programs cover such geographical areas as Africa, Latin America and the Asia–Pacific.

Global corporatisation and museum franchising provide new avenues for international engagements and bring a museum to a new level of global outreach. However, it is not clear if these new practices facilitate cultural diplomacy. Can global expansion strategies give birth to a new type of museum diplomacy? Can such a diplomacy be defined by institutional commitments and mission on the world stage, rather than being shaped by government agenda? There are no simple answers to these questions. This book, however, takes up the challenge to address them.

The book was inspired by the growing power and multiplying effects of global expansion strategies, pioneered by Guggenheim but adopted across museums from different countries. Though severely criticised, both in academia and in the professional museum world, for sacrificing art scholarship for economic returns, Guggenheim's bold practices in global corporatisation and franchising have significantly influenced the development of museum agency across countries (Baudelle 2015). For example, "franchised museums pursuing global economies of scale and size (Tate, Pompidou, Getty, Paley Center, Reina Sofia, Imperial War, Louvre, Hermitage, Caixaforum or Ludwig) have multiplied with varying degrees of success" (Guerzoni 2015,

190). Moreover, museum emulations of the McGuggenisation formula were rapidly erected in countries and regions beyond the Western hemisphere, including such parts of the world as "BRICS (Brazil, Russia, India, China and South Africa), the Orient and the Middle East, in Central and South America and in the former Soviet Bloc republics" (Guerzoni 2015, 190).

This book explores two particular cases of post-Guggenheim developments that evidence a successful adoption – or perhaps it is better to say adaptation – of the global expansion model of museums in China and Russia. First, to trace the development of global corporatisation practices among museums, the book offers the unique case of the K11 Art Mall, opened in Hong Kong in 2008 by Chinese billionaire Adrian Cheng. As the first fully retail-oriented museum in the world, K11 employs a new art-commerce business franchise model. K11 branches are speedily spreading across China and already cover almost 1.5 million square metres of total floor area across shopping malls (K11 2018). K11 aims to bring arts to the masses by redefining shopping experiences and creating opportunities for the growth and global promotion of contemporary Chinese arts.

Reflecting on the example of Guggenheim, Cheng explained: "K11 shares the same view as the Guggenheim Museum Foundation. Instead of waiting for people to come to a dedicated art museum, we bring art to the general public by opening up more channels where they could see art" (Cheng 2018). The global ambition of K11, however, goes beyond merely winning Chinese markets. Funded by K11 revenues, the non-profit K11 Art Foundation has been implementing large-scale international art programs, curatorial residencies and experimental projects with overseas museums. Aiming to promote contemporary Chinese artists on the global level, the international activities of the K11 Art Foundation directly contribute to China's current foreign policy agenda for rebranding its cultural image on the world stage.

Second, to demonstrate productive deployment of cultural franchising, the book explores the International Network of Foundations developed by the State Hermitage Museum. One of the largest and well-recognised museums in the world, with three million objects in a collection representing different civilisations across time and space, the Hermitage enjoys a dedicated place among such universal museums as the British Museum in London, the Metropolitan Museum of Art in New York and the Louvre in Paris. Since the 1990s, the Hermitage has been developing a powerful network of cultural foundations in different corners of the world. The network now numbers a dozen foundations and museum branches across North America, Europe and the Middle East and is also expanding to Asia. The development of this network has been to a certain degree empowered and encouraged by the Guggenheim experience in global franchising.

The first joint franchise, between the Hermitage and Guggenheim, was the hybrid Guggenheim–Hermitage that opened in Las Vegas in October 2001. It was followed by another attempt to build a new branch in Vilnius seven years later. Even though both cross-institutional franchise projects proved unsustainable, the director of the Hermitage does not consider these experiments to be failures and recollects the time of joint activities with special sympathy. We "have travelled to Singapore and various places. We're ready to participate everywhere [. . .] to obtain a unique cultural effect (Kishkovsky 2009)."

The Guggenheim–Hermitage Museum was a robust platform on which we could "carry out our research work, create a new model for collaboration in the field of culture and continue to fulfil our main mission" (Gibson 2003, 22). The Hermitage International Network of Foundations has a distinct diplomatic ambition. It helps the museum pursue its commitments to establishing and sustaining "strong cultural ties and collaborative cultural relations" throughout Russia and the rest of the world by providing dedicated channels for Russian cultural diplomacy (Piotrovsky 2017).

These cases from China and Russia do more than offer captivating examples of how the Guggenheim's global expansion models were successfully adopted and further transformed by museums beyond the Western world. More importantly, these examples evidence the emergence of new alternative avenues of museum diplomacy that no longer depend on government commissions to serve immediate geopolitical interests. As the book further illustrates, both Russian and Chinese cases of museum global expansion shape a new generation of museum diplomacy in the twenty-first century. The book identifies these alternative pathways of contemporary museum diplomacy to explore how it works and what challenges and opportunities it brings to museums.

Methodological adventures: from desk research to immersive auto-ethnography

The empirical framework of the book is twofold. First, it closely analyses global expansion strategies employed by Guggenheim under the leadership of Thomas Krens. He is a legendary person who is well known for transforming the museum into a truly transnational enterprise. These explorations help to provide scope for and to outline key characteristics of museum franchising and global corporatisation to interrogate their role and place in contemporary museum diplomacy. The book explores the wider context of the Guggenheim's institutional history, philosophy, organisational behaviour, financial sustainability and global partnerships. An in-depth institutional analysis is based on qualitative research, including the analysis of online informational resources and annual organisational reports (1977–2010) as well as U.S.

Internal Revenue Service (IRS) reports. IRS reports such as Form 990, collected from 2001 to 2012, were particularly instrumental in analysing the Guggenheim's operational budget. They helped to identify external funding sources and explore the structure and composition of the museum's Board of Trustees as well as its transformations through time.

Also, the book offers unique insights from management staff of the Guggenheim Museum in New York and one of the former branches of the Guggenheim, the Deutsche Guggenheim in Berlin, Germany. I collected these internal perspectives through interviews conducted 2010–2012, when I commenced my doctorate research on the phenomenon of the Guggenheim. I was lucky to talk in person with Joan Young, Director of Curatorial Affairs, and Laura Miller, Director of the Marketing Department. In addition, I talked with Sara Bernshausen, the Associate Gallery Manager at Deutsche Guggenheim. These interviews clarified important nuances and details of the Guggenheim's activities on the global stage and provided an invaluable contribution to the analysis in this book. My attempts to interview Thomas Krens to get more personal insight into his visions for the revolutionary transformations of the museum were, unfortunately, unsuccessful. However, he is quite an outspoken person and has always been very open about sharing his opinion in the media. Drawing on these media interviews, I have been able to piece together Krens's management philosophy, which turned the museum into a global franchise.

The book applies global expansion models to case studies from non-Western contexts, such as the Hermitage Museum in Russia and K11 from China. These cases of museum franchising and global corporatisation identify and explain the direct implications of new practices for contemporary cultural diplomacy. They provide empirical evidence to the main arguments of this book, which seeks to identify and explain a new type of museum diplomacy. This diplomacy redefines the traditional relationship between national governments, museums and other stakeholders by seeing museums as key players in diplomacy.

However, to uncover the motivations, reasoning and logic behind museum franchising and global corporatisation employed by museums in China and Russia, a document analysis was not enough. Exploring less transparent environments within more authoritarian political regimes in China and Russia required a full immersion in the context of museums, their activities and networks. My methods comprised an ethnographic trip to China in summer 2018, and even my personal auto-ethnographic experience of volunteering for the Hermitage Museum Foundations in New York (2010) and London (2011).

My ethnographic research in China included immersive observations of the interior design, audiences and activities and exhibitions of two K11 Art Mall branches in Shanghai and Hong Kong. Moreover, it incorporated numerous interviews with a wide body of respondents, who I recruited by employing a snowballing approach. It was not easy to find the right people to talk to, due to both language barriers (especially in Shanghai) and the local political culture and environment. I needed to actively engage with my personal connections to find ways to reach out to people working for K11. These new acquaintances were important for me to expand my network and connect to more relevant people among the huge K11 community of employees and top management.

However, I was lucky enough to progress in my recruiting adventures to interview Venus Lau, the Artistic Director of the K11 Art Foundation based in Shanghai, as well as Ross Leo, the Executive Director of the Foundation in Hong Kong. Furthermore, I convinced Adrian Cheng, the leader and founder of K11, to respond to my questions via email, after multiple online conversations with his numerous assistants. These interviews were very helpful in illuminating the institutional ambitions of K11 to play the key role on the global stage in promoting contemporary Chinese arts and projecting a Chinese cultural image.

While I also personally met with and interviewed an army of lower staff managers at K11, including curators, marketing and public relations officers, receptionists and guides, these interviews proved less informative. In most cases, K11 employees strictly conformed to the institutional perspective and were reluctant to share any personal viewpoints that might deviate from the official institutional position. I ended up interviewing various respondents outside K11 in order to piece together the complex puzzle of the retail-based museum phenomenon and its role on the global stage. My interviewees included emerging, well-established and internationally recognised artists, museum scholars and researchers, cultural practitioners and museum workers from other private and public institutions. It even included students who had previously interned for K11. The majority of them, of course, opted to be anonymous respondents, as it was the only way for me to lure out some illuminating nuances, critical perspectives and missing details.

My research into the State Hermitage had a different but similar approach. On the one hand, I could rely on a large body of documentation produced by the Hermitage Foundations in different countries, including annual Foundation reports as well as various project and program reports. In particular, I was able to rely on annual reports and newsletters of the State Hermitage Museum Foundation U.S.A. (2010–2015) and U.K. (2010–2015). Qualitative analysis of these documents helped to explore in more detail the activities, stakeholders, audiences and budgets of these non-profit institutions over recent years. Apart from the analysis of this official institutional perspective, I drew on my personal volunteer experience in London and Washington D.C., during which I took on such roles as Communication Associate and D.C. Event Coordinator.

In 2010–2011, my volunteer engagements were not intended to gain experience for the purpose of this book. In fact, as an international graduate student in both countries, I was attracted by the opportunity to be part of the Hermitage family while away from home. Through this experience, I was able to connect to my Russian culture and heritage and share it with my new overseas friends and colleagues. However, it was also the time I first observed and realised the power of the museum's global networks to establish strong connections with local audiences, engage wealthy stakeholders, consolidate diaspora communities and implement a great number of international exchange projects.

I was lucky to work hand in hand with the then-Director of the Foundation in the U.S., Masha Tolstoy Sarandinaki, the American-born great-granddaughter of the famous Russian writer Leo Tolstoy. My work was also supervised by Paul Rodzianko, Chairman of the Foundation (2007–2015). He is a wealthy philanthropist who has supported numerous Russian cultural organisations and projects in the U.S.

In London, I had the opportunity to work with Dr Thierry Morel, then-Director of the Foundation U.K., and Geraldine Norman, Chief Executive of the U.K. Foundation. Norman not only has served on the Foundation since its inception but is also a dedicated Hermitage historian. She spent many years in Saint Petersburg researching and has published two books about the history of the Hermitage. It was Norman who personally introduced me to Dr Mikhail Piotrovsky, the legendary Director of the Hermitage Museum, when he was in London on one of his diplomatic visits.

Despite this personal connection, it was not possible to catch Piotrovsky for an interview due to his busy travelling schedule, which kept him on the move across countries and continents on various missions. However, this book offers invaluable insights from Katia Sirakanian, Head of the Development Department of the State Hermitage Museum, who was interviewed in May 2017. This interview clarified important nuances of the museum's global expansion strategy, which has seen them successfully reach out to new, powerful and wealthy supporters in many countries around the world.

As these insights reveal, my methodological approaches combined traditional desk research with adventurous and international travel experiences. It was a decade-long journey that led to the development of this book and generously provided multiple opportunities to observe the emergence of the phenomenon of museum global expansion. It also offered authentic experiences to learn how we can discuss and explain this phenomenon.

Conceptual foundations and the design of the book

The main goal of the book is to provide a fresh perspective on museum franchising and global corporatisation. Both of these practices have been previously discussed, predominantly in relation to Guggenheim and, in most cases, in terms of imperialistic McDonaldisation. For example, the Guggenheim's international activities have been severely criticised in both the media and academic literature as a manifestation of neo-colonial powers, or even as an aggressive expansion of cultural imperialism (Rauen 2001; Sorkin 2005). Guggenheim was accused of being a "superpower hegemon, seducing locals into paying through their noses for the 'privilege' of having its brand and its protection" (Sylvester 2009, 120).

Acknowledging the political implications of the Guggenheim's global expansion model, this book aims to go beyond an imperialistic reading of these new practices. It situates global corporatisation and museum franchising within a cultural diplomacy framework to find a new language for these museum innovations. As one of the first publications in the "Museums in Focus" series, this book offers a new approach that questions, analyses and explains the global expansion models that shape international trends in museum diplomacy. The book contributes to the key goals of the series by facilitating a debate across disciplines. It employs the framework of contemporary cultural diplomacy to reconceptualise Guggenheim's international activities and its transformations in the context of other museums across countries.

Cultural diplomacy is still a contested academic field and a "relatively uncharted territory" that exists across more consolidated disciplines, including political science, international relations and public communication (Goff 2013; Lamonica and Isernia 2016; McConnell et al. 2012). The book builds on the foundational developments of the current diplomacy scholarship and focuses on two key aspects that challenge traditional forms of museum diplomacy. The first aspect is the appearance of powerful non-state actors that increasingly intervene in diplomatic activities among nation states. Second, the book finds a way to accommodate a more nuanced exploration of contemporary cultural diplomacy that no longer fits the narrow paradigm of government-led activities. To do this, it employs Joseph Nye's (2004) theory of soft power, which refers to the ability of a country to achieve its foreign policy objectives through persuasion and attraction.

In an age of increasing globalisation, new technologies and access to international resources have significantly empowered new diplomatic players. In pursuit of their own institutional interests and commitments, these non-state players take a more autonomous role on the global stage. They also enjoy a much wider reach to audiences and constituencies across borders and acquire powers to shape global discourses, set international agendas and communicate messages of political significance (Habermas 2001; Kelley 2010, 2014). However, these actors earn their diplomatic legitimacy not through their official status, like governmental players, but rather through their capabilities to raise their own budget to go global, to offer professional expertise in addressing international issues and to earn credibility in the eyes of the global publics (Avant et al. 2010). As a result, these actors can develop their global reputation, recognition and visibility when they start to project their own soft power.

Within Nye's power typologies, ranging from the hard power of military might to the multilateral diplomacy of institutional structuration, soft power is understood as a more advanced and sophisticated tool for achieving foreign policy objectives by simply seducing other actors or influencing "others to get the outcomes one wants" (Nye 2004, 2). Nye argues that this type of power offers an alternative solution to address the complexity of international relations by employing culture as the foundation of international influence on other societies. In recent years, the term soft power has been employed not only to describe the ability of a country to influence the behaviour of other states but also to refer to an institutional capacity to generate the power of attractiveness to achieve organisational goals in a broader international environment (Kenta et al. 2016).

This book explores this institutional soft power in relation to contemporary museums. It expands an emerging museum studies scholarship that only recently started to define museums as "networked civil society institutions with soft power." The soft power of museums could be understood as an ability to "amplify civic discourse, accelerate cultural change, and contribute to cultural intelligence among the great diversity of city dwellers, visitors, policy makers and leaders" (Lord and Blankenberg 2015, 19). The book explores museums as non-state actors of diplomacy leveraging their powers on the global stage. Museums do this through developing complex constituent networks, liberating their cross-cultural engagements from financial dependency on their nation states. At the same time, the book aims to demonstrate that by generating this institutional soft power, museums build their global reputation, expertise and credibility for representing national cultures abroad and contributing to state efforts in cultural diplomacy.

Chapter 1, "Cultural Diplomacy of a Different Kind," establishes the conceptual foundation of the book. It elaborates on two key aspects of the global political climate in which states, international organisations and non-state actors become more "integrated into the complex, multi-faceted patterns of world politics" (Hocking et al. 2012, 18). The chapter explores the foundational principles of non-state legitimacy and relates them to museums' international activities. It also expands the framework of museum diplomacy by integrating the concept of institutional soft power to explain cases in which diplomacy draws primarily on museum leadership, as opposed to governmental initiatives. Furthermore, the chapter defines boundaries of cultural diplomacy in relation to other terms and concepts that are frequently used interchangeably with museum diplomacy.

These conceptual foundations inform the following two chapters of the book, which illustrate exactly how these principles work through specific case studies. These specific chapters focus on two different global expansion strategies successfully trialled by Guggenheim and further transformed by K11 and the Hermitage Museum.

Chapter 2, "Museum Diplomacy as a Corporate Enterprise," explores corporate partnerships and museum commercialisation as implemented by Guggenheim. It further traces the transformation of these practices in the context of contemporary China by exploring more closely the case of K11 Art Mall. The chapter discusses the unintentional contributions of Guggenheim to projecting American liberal democracy and the freedom of the market economy. But it also reveals that the Guggenheim's international programming has a stronger institutional focus and agenda, placing it outside of cultural diplomacy activities. The diplomatic manifestation of the global corporatisation practice is, nevertheless, identified through a close analysis of K11 international activities. In this way, the chapter documents the emergence of powerful private actors of diplomacy among museums in an authoritarian regime such as China. K11 offers a convincing case that demonstrates the power of private diplomacy to represent national arts and culture in the global arena.

Chapter 3, "Museum Diplomacy as a Global Franchise," investigates the structure, rationale and design of transnational museum networks in the context of two museums. This chapter aims to demonstrate how franchising strategy, first pioneered by Guggenheim, has re-emerged in the International Network of the Hermitage Museum Foundations. The network empowered the museum to go global without the traditional patronage of the Russian government. First, the chapter explores the birth of the Guggenheim franchising model, its rapid development at the beginning of the twenty-first century and its gradual decline in recent years. While demonstrating the direct implications of the museum's global branding, the chapter questions whether the Guggenheim's branches abroad could facilitate cultural diplomacy. However, the case of the Hermitage reveals that cultural franchising can create a global infrastructure for non-state cultural diplomacy. The Hermitage International Network provides a unique example of highly effective museum diplomacy that outperforms the Russian government in its international outreach and impact.

Comparing and contrasting three cases of global expansion practices and their implications for cultural diplomacy, the book offers new insights into the development and transformation of museum diplomacy in the era of globalisation. It illustrates that museums are becoming important centres of soft power, and their international brands, presence and visibility allow them to implement transnational projects and programs with strong diplomatic agendas and significance. While the case of the Guggenheim, in the context of the U.S. only, interrogates global museum practices to pave the way for contemporary cultural diplomacy, the case studies of Russian and Chinese museums prove these to be key dimensions of museum diplomacy in the twenty-first century.

References

Alexander, Victoria. 1999. A Delicate Balance: Museums and the Market-Place. *Museum International* 51(2): 29–34.

Arndt, Richard. 2005. *First Resort of Kings: American Cultural Diplomacy in the 20th Century*. Washington, DC: Potomac Books.

Avant, Deborah, Finnemore, Martha and Susan Sell. 2010. *Who Governs the Globe?* Cambridge: Cambridge University Press.

Baudelle, Guy. 2015. The New Louvre in Lens: A Regionally Embedded National Project. *European Planning Studies* 23(8): 1476–1493.

Cheng, Adrian. 2018. Interview by Natalia Grincheva.

Cockcroft, Eva. 1985. Abstract Expressionism, Weapon of the Cold War. In *Polock and After: The Critical Debate*, ed. Francis Frascina, 147–154. New York, NY: Routledge.

Cummings, Milton. 2003. *Cultural Diplomacy and the United States Government: A Survey*. Cultural Diplomacy Research Series. Worthington, DC: Americans for the Arts.

de Hart Mathews, Jane. 1976. Art and Politics in Cold War America. *American Historical Review* 81(4): 762–787.

Dicke, Thomas. 1992. *Franchising in America: The Development of a Business Method, 1840–1980*. Chapel Hill, NC: UNC Press Books.

Digout, Amy. 2006. *Courting the West: Nicholas I, Cultural Diplomacy and the State Hermitage Museum in 1852*. Montreal: McGill University Press.

Fraser, Andrea. 2006. Isn't This a Wonderful Place? (A Tour of a Tour of the Guggenheim Bilbao). In *Museum Frictions*, eds. Ivan Karp and Corinne Kratz, 135–160. Durham, NC: Duke University Press.

Gibson, Stuart. 2003. The Hermitage and Institutional Change: A Leap into the Twenty-first Century. *Museum International* 55(1): 20–26.

Goff, Patricia. 2013. Cultural Diplomacy. In *The Oxford Handbook of Modern Diplomacy*, eds. Andrew Cooper, Jorge Heine and Ramesh Thakur. Oxford: Oxford University Press.

Grincheva, Natalia. 2016. Museum Dimension of American "Soft Power": Genealogy of Cultural Diplomacy Institutions. In *"Hearts and Minds": US Cultural Management in Foreign Relations in the 21st Century*, ed. Matthew Chambers, 125–164. Frankfurt am Main: Peter Lang.

Grincheva, Natalia. 2017. Sustainable Fundraising in the 21st Century: Behind the Scenes of the Global Guggenheim Success. In *Systems Thinking in Museums: Theory and Practice*, eds. Yuha Jung and Ann Love, 181–190. Lanham, MD: Rowman & Littlefield.

Guerzoni, Guido. 2015. The Museum Building Boom. In *Museums, Cities and Soft Power*, eds. Gail Lord and Ngaire Blankenberg, 187–198. Washington, DC: American Association of Museums.

Habermas, Jurgen. 2001. *The Postnational Constellation*. Cambridge, MA: The MIT Press.

Hobbs, Stuart. 1997. *The End of American Avant Garde*. New York, NY: New York University Press.

Hocking, Brian, Melissen, Jan, Riordan, Shaun and Paul Sharp. 2012. *Integrative Diplomacy in the 21st Century*. Netherlands Institute of International Relations.

K11. 2018. About Us. www.k11.com (accessed July 2018).

Kelley, John. 2010. The New Diplomacy: Evolution of a Revolution. *Diplomacy & Statecraft* 21: 286–305.

Kelley, John. 2014. *Agency Change*. Lanham, MD: Rowman & Littlefield.

Kenta, Michael, Sommerfeldtb, Erich J. and Adam J. Saffer. 2016. Social Networks, Power, and Public Relations: Tertius Iungens as a Cocreational Approach to Studying Relationship Networks. *Public Relations Review* 42(1): 91–100.

Kishkovsky, Sophia. 2009. Building a Greater Hermitage. *Art News*, 1 September.

Lamonica, Alessandro G. and Pierangelo Isernia. 2016. *Cultural Diplomacy as Discipline and Practice: Concepts, Training, and Skills*. European Union National Institutes for Culture.

Lord, Gail and Ngaire Blankenberg. 2015. *Museums, Cities and Soft Power*. Washington, DC: American Association of Museums.

MacGregor, Neil. 2004. Museums of the World: The British Museum. *ICOM News* 1: 2–3.

McConnell, Fiona, Moreau, Terri and Jason Dittmer. 2012. Mimicking State Diplomacy: The Legitimizing Strategies of Unofficial Diplomacies. *Geoforum* 43: 804–814.

Ninkovich, Frank. 1997. The Currents of Cultural Diplomacy: Art and the State Department, 1938–1947. *Diplomatic History* 1(1): 215–238.

Nye, Joseph. 2004. *Soft Power: The Means to Success in World Politics*. New York, NY: Public Affairs.

Piotrovsky, Mikhail. 2017. Art above Politics. Hermitage Museum Foundation, USA. http://bit.ly/2fXwdty (accessed July 2018).

Rauen, Marjorie. 2001. Reflections on the Space of Flows: The Guggenheim Museum Bilbao. *The Journal of Arts Management, Law, and Society* 30(4): 283–300.

Sorkin, Michael. 2005. Brand Aid or the Lexus and the Guggenheim (Further Tales of the Notorious B.I.G.ness). In *Commodification and Spectacle in Architecture*, ed. William Saunders, 22–33. Minneapolis, MN: University of Minnesota Press.

Sylvester, Christine. 2009. *Art/Museums: International Relations Where We Least Expect It*. London: Paradigm Publishers.

Trilupaityte, Skaidra. 2009. Guggenheim's Global Travel and the Appropriation of a National Avant-Garde for Cultural Planning in Vilnius. *International Journal of Cultural Policy* 15(1): 123–138.

1 Cultural diplomacy of a different kind

This chapter places international museum activities within the current diplomacy literature. It applies a framework of non-state diplomacy and non-state legitimacy to the context of museums. It also establishes strong boundaries between cultural diplomacy and a wide range of terms that are frequently invoked in discussions about museum diplomacy, including cultural relations, nation branding and soft power. This distinction has proven useful in the context of the book. It helps to differentiate museums' international engagements between those that we can confidently call cultural diplomacy and those that fall outside of diplomatic activities. The main goal of the chapter is to develop an analytical framework of museum diplomacy with clearly defined characteristics and principles of operation. This framework guides the development of key arguments throughout the following case studies.

Cultural diplomacy received status as an official state activity in the midst of the Cold War between the United States (U.S.) and the Soviet Union during the twentieth century. Initially, it was defined by the U.S. Department of State in 1959 as "the direct and enduring contact between people of different nations [. . .] to help create a better climate of international trust and understanding in which official relations can operate" (U.S. Department of State 1969, iv). Since then, cultural diplomacy has been mainly employed as a form of strategic cross-cultural communication between countries. While it has always relied on people-to-people exchanges to establish bridges of mutual trust, the design of programs and funding matters have remained a prerogative of national governments (Schneider 2003).

However, an era of expanding globalisation and rapid technological progress has increased global mobility and the circulation of capital, labour and information. This new, complex international climate has progressively challenged traditional models of diplomatic communication. In the past, these were closed, predicted and controlled by official diplomats. Now, international communication is becoming more transparent and more exposed to global publics (Hocking et al. 2012; Melissen 2005). The classical model of bilateral relations between states has been replaced by a new diplomacy. This diplomacy is based on poly-lateral communication among a wide range of actors leading to a growing dissolution of the absolute powers of nation states (Jora 2013, 46).

Since the 1990s, the state monopoly on diplomacy has been gradually declining. Instead, the field of international relations has seen the appearance of new, non-state actors who "have global interests and the will to make them felt on the world stage" (Kleiner 2008; La Porte 2012, 1; Melissen 2005; Potter 2002; Spiro 2013). Non-state actors can be defined as "non-sovereign entities that exercise significant economic, political, or social power and influence on the national or international levels" (La Porte 2012, 4). Non-state diplomacy is based on these actors' capabilities as opposed to diplomacy of status. In many cases, non-state actors do not have legal status to represent their states. However, they can acquire diplomatic capabilities and sources of legitimate representation that make them key actors in the field of diplomacy (Kelley 2014).

Based on a large body of diplomacy literature that explores sources of non-state legitimacy, three important components of actors' capabilities stay recurrent across different scholars (Avant et al. 2010; Barnett and Finnemore 2005; Edwards 1999; Kelley 2010; La Porte 2012). They include (1) *expertise*, which refers to the strong global reputation of an organisation; (2) *credibility*, or the ability of an organisation to establish long-term trustful relationships with global audiences; and (3) *resources and alliances*, which point to an institutional capacity to generate funding for its global activities. The following sections apply these capabilities to contemporary museums in order to define these institutions as legitimate actors of cultural diplomacy. This definition helps to unfold the main arguments of the book, which sees museums in the twenty-first century as economically viable players with recognised cultural expertise and credibility in the eyes of the foreign publics to lead cultural diplomacy activities.

Museums as diplomacy experts

Expertise of non-state actors refers to a specialised professional knowledge on issues of global public concern. It also draws on the efficiency of these actors in implementing international projects (Reinalda and Verbeek 2001, 150). To establish expertise on a global level, an organisation has to find a way to differentiate itself among a wide range of players. It can do this by excelling at its core competency such that, ideally, it is in high demand with a relatively low supply (Mitchell 2014, 82). Organisations with recognised expertise grow their global reputation by leading international programs while preserving their autonomy against other powerful stakeholders.

Expertise makes non-state actors competitive in the global environment, in some cases to such an extent that they outperform their national governments. In contrast to highly bureaucratic and slow government organisations, non-state actors are usually very dynamic. They are more adaptive and highly responsive to innovations and changes in an unpredictable international climate (Jora 2013, 36). These qualities make non-state actors powerful enough to intervene in complex diplomatic situations, when governments fail to act in a timely manner, to resolve difficult issues.

In the museum world, a good example is the leadership of Neil MacGregor, former Director of the British Museum. On behalf of the museum, MacGregor mediated high-level diplomatic situations to provide first aid to cultural institutions and communities in the midst of major international conflicts. For example, during the Iraq War, which started in 2003, when the U.S. and British allies invaded the country, it was the British Museum that saved Iraq's main repository of national archaeological treasures from complete destruction. In the mass chaos of the raid, the Iraq National Museum was descended upon by looters and "gangs [. . .] carrying away what they could and smashing what they could not" (*Telegraph* 2011). MacGregor telephoned the prime minister of Great Britain, who had U.S. tanks deployed in front of the museum to secure it. During the following week, British Museum curators travelled to Baghdad to help their Iraqi colleagues with conservation and preservation tasks and provided first aid to recover museum resources.

This case demonstrates the strong power of the British Museum to directly intervene in official diplomatic relations among countries in a complex international context. It also points to the ability of the museum to fill the gap in the diplomatic climate that occurs when government actors fail to work proactively. This ability draws on the cultural expertise of a museum that owns one of the world's largest and most diverse collections, stretching across times and civilisations. This colonial heritage has always given the museum leverage and the power to position itself and act on the world stage as a cultural ambassador. The museum pursues its ambition to represent "the world under one roof" (MacGregor 2012, 39) by actively involving itself in contemporary cultural and geopolitical issues (Binns 2005). This diplomacy on the part of the British Museum is a strategic pathway for retaining its institutional legitimacy in the context of ongoing acrimonious debates that demand the return of the world's greatest treasures, currently in the museum's possession, to their homelands.

Obviously, this diplomacy is based on the institutional privilege as well, as it is a result of the museum's imperial colonial legacy. Nevertheless, the cultural expertise of the British Museum as it outperforms government efforts in complex diplomatic situations is undeniable. Another good example of this is the 2005 blockbuster exhibition "Forgotten Empire: The World of Ancient Persia." This exhibition aimed to mitigate political tension between the U.K. and Iran. While President Mahmoud Ahmadinejad rejected British offers of economic concessions in return for an end to nuclear activities, national institutions in Tehran loaned art treasures to the British Museum. This act of diplomacy aimed to tell meaningful stories about the Persian Empire during 550–330 BC under the Achaemenid Great Kings, in order to facilitate a better understanding of Iran culture, history and identity (Hoggard 2006). This case also demonstrates the strong reputation of the British Museum among its international colleagues to lead cross-cultural initiatives that address urgent diplomatic matters.

Museums earn their diplomatic expertise by employing cultural knowledge as a foundational means of communicating to, understanding and appreciating the other. This approach allows them to humanise complex issues in the international political environment and to project a high level of institutional credibility in the eyes of its foreign constituency.

Museums as institutions of trust

Credibility, as a significant source of diplomatic capabilities, is based on building strong connections and trustful relationships with a direct constituency. Non-state actors can leverage their legitimacy because they are able to exploit their mobility, flexibility and less centralised organisational structure to better communicate with the public (Kelley 2010, 289). Specifically, the dependence of non-state actors on public support impels them to excel at their communication strategies and improve the quality of their messaging (La Porte 2012). Non-state actors demonstrate strong advantages over more official diplomats because they usually establish closer ties with the public and thus can better serve the populations they claim to represent (Kelley 2014; Melissen 2006; Snow 2009). As a result, non-state actors often have greater credibility than governments "precisely because they have a better understanding of the citizens' concerns and deal with them more effectively" (La Porte 2012, 10).

In the twenty-first century, many governments have recognised the power of non-state credibility. For example, in the U.S., citizen or backyard diplomacy is well promoted by the State Department to encourage the non-profit art sector to take the lead in cross-cultural engagements and to serve as a diplomatic force on behalf of the country. "The American people are some of our nation's best ambassadors," former President George W. Bush used to say. "We must find ways to utilize their talents and skills more effectively

[. . .] and we need more of our citizens involved in our public diplomacy" (U.S. Department of State Archive 2005).

On the one hand, this government approach to backyard diplomacy is rather instrumental. It aims to capitalise on citizens' ability to build trustful relationships with other countries in order to achieve foreign policy goals. On the other hand, it delegates power to the public sector, demonstrating that "informal diplomacy is becoming ever more important than formalized institutions" (Vezirgiannidou 2013, 636). However, an excessive guardianship of citizen diplomacy undermines its credibility and destroys a positive image of involved actors (Scott-Smith 2009, 52). Cultural exchanges motivated by direct government interests transform these initiatives into a form of government propaganda (Jenkins 2009).

Within the context of American museums, government involvement in cross-cultural activities has always been a matter of controversy. A good example is the Museum Connect Program (2007–2017), funded by the U.S. government and administered by the American Alliance of Museums (AAM) to implement museum diplomacy across countries. Through this program, American museums receive government awards of up to $100,000 to work in collaboration with foreign museum partners. These partnerships aimed to celebrate "art, history, cultural preservation and science exchanges," bringing people together to foster greater understanding (U.S. Department of State 2012).

In 2007, when the program was first opened, National Public Radio immediately questioned its credibility, interrogating whether American museums really "want to be used to promote foreign policy," building on "the Marshall Plan" (Blair 2007). Lee Rosenbaum, who writes for the *Wall Street Journal* and *New York Times*, criticised the program: "cultural ties can assuredly improve relations between countries, but not when they are conceived as an instrument of political propaganda. AAM has done a disservice to its members by signing up for this dubious government-curated enterprise" (Rosenbaum 2007).

This civil society discourse around government practices in cultural diplomacy not only proves academic claims in favour of the power of non-state credibility but also reveals that museums are expected to act autonomously from the control of the national government. The credibility of museums as non-state actors of diplomacy rests on their reputation for serving up arts and culture rather than promoting national ideologies. However, to pursue their institutional cultural missions, museums need to secure funding for their global activities. To stay independent from political influence, non-state actors need to build their own *resources and alliances*, ensuring they can sustain their operations in the international context.

Museums in the global economic sector of culture

Diversified sources of income from multiple stakeholders can minimise and even eliminate the economic dependency of organisations on national governments (Mitchell 2014). Private or corporate donors help non-profit institutions, including museums, to build autonomy from strong political pressure and direct control of the government.

Private museum diplomacy, though, is not new, particularly in the U.S., where most museums were founded by wealthy philanthropists (Arndt 2005). In comparison to European museums, established under the auspice of government forces, U.S. museums have grown from the ground up, created by individuals and families to celebrate and commemorate personal legacies. The American public museum "is a monument to the powerful men who not only led the development of American finance capitalism, but also understood its cultural and ideological needs" (Duncan 1995, 70). Even in the context of the Cold War, private forces played a key role in sustaining museum diplomacy in the U.S.

For example, multiple shows of American Expressionism toured around the world under the strong leadership of its supporter and private philanthropist Nelson Rockefeller (Guilbaut 2005). Exclusively private sources, or "Rockefeller's deep pockets overturned the gradualist thinking of the founders of cultural diplomacy" (Arndt 2005, 363). It was with Rockefeller's support and help that the idea of a "museum without walls" came into reality. Since 1946, he has empowered many American museums to go international and engage more closely with their foreign counterparts through international exchange programs (Arndt 2005, 364).

Among more recent examples is the Rubin Museum of Himalayan Art in New York (Goff 2013). It was established by Shelley and Donald Rubin to offer comprehensive programming on Himalayan art, culture and religion by making accessible their private collections. Without support from the governments of Bhutan or Nepal, the museum "promotes understanding, and inspires personal connections to the ideas, cultures, and art of Himalayan Asia" (RMA 2004). "Arguably, those governments would not be able to achieve what the Rubins have achieved, insulated from the politics of promoting national culture" (Goff 2013, 427). Rubin's private philanthropy, with international vision and missions that create platforms for a cross-cultural dialogue and exchanges, establishes alternative avenues for museum diplomacy.

While private philanthropic support remains strong in the museum sector, in the twenty-first century museums are experimenting with new ways to sustain expensive operations across borders. Corporate sponsorship is another channel of support for implementing large-scale international programs. For example, in the U.K., British Petroleum, the global oil and gas giant, has long been a major sponsor of many of Britain's principal museums. It has in particular favoured grand international blockbusters that can attract larger audiences (Miller 2014).

A good illustration is the 2016 British Museum's blockbuster "Sunken Cities: Egypt's Lost Worlds," which showcased two ancient cities discovered on the coast of Alexandria in the Nile Delta. This exhibition offered the global public new insights into Egyptian heritage that had been hidden from the public for centuries. However, it also provided a platform for British Petroleum to pursue its corporate interests in its Egyptian gas projects. This exhibit continues a series of long-lasting corporate relationships in which British Petroleum collaborates with the British Museum to gain access to policymakers in other countries – in Mexico or Australia, for example, where the oil company has ongoing oil interests (Johnson 2016).

Corporate sponsorship remains rather controversial in the world of museums and receives a considerable amount of criticism. The direct interests of involved stakeholders to a certain degree affect curatorial, marketing and communication decisions in museums. For example, "in order to meet sponsors' expectations, museums gravitate toward exhibition[s] that guarantee to be popular" (Dilevko and Gottlieb 2004, 31). However, to balance the institutional reputation and comply with ethical norms and expectations, museums can leverage their funding sources. First, they can strategically choose among private or corporate benefactors. Second, museums can decide how much they can take from each of them.

Securing "a high proportion of funds from a large number of private individuals" or corporate sponsors usually ensures a healthier balance (Mitchell 2014, 83). Adopting these strategies, museums can build a more autonomous position on the world stage while remaining free from ideological government control. Furthermore, museum franchising, pioneered by Guggenheim, provides a new avenue for delivering collections and exhibitions across national borders. More and more, museums around the world are adopting a franchising model to establish new branches across countries and continents.

In addition to such famous cases as Hermitage Amsterdam (2004), Louvre Abu Dhabi (2017) and Centre Pompidou Shanghai (2019), there is also Science Gallery International. It opened in 2008 in Dublin at Trinity College "to pioneer creative collisions between art and science." In only few years, the gallery has rapidly grown into a global network (SGI 2018). Only a decade after its inception, the Global Science Gallery Network has acquired six branches across four continents, including satellites in London, Melbourne, Bengaluru, Venice and Detroit. The network boasts of engaging

1,200 scientists, artists and researchers from different countries through ground-breaking exhibitions and international tours.

Not only does the Global Science Gallery Network successfully emulate the Guggenheim franchise idea but, more importantly, it also demonstrates that in an era of increasing globalisation, a new generation of museums actively employs global expansion models of operations. These practices allow them to reach wider audiences across borders and draw on artistic creativity, cultural resources and financial support across multiple local communities in different countries. But what is the relevance of these international engagements to contemporary cultural diplomacy? Global resources and the activities and ambitions of new players "do not necessarily make them diplomats" (Kleiner 2008, 341).

This book analyses whether cultural franchising or global corporatisation can offer museums new avenues to exercise cultural diplomacy. To answer this, it is important to draw clear boundaries between what cultural diplomacy is and what it is not. However, this task is quite challenging. Defined as a cross-cultural "exchange of ideas, information, art, and other aspects of culture" (Cummings 2003, 1), cultural diplomacy provides a wide and inclusive framework that makes a broad range of cultural activities an easy fit.

Many scholars point to growing confusion around an interdisciplinary and under-theorised concept of cultural diplomacy (Gilboa 2008; Goff 2013; Melissen 2005). On the top of this, the term is frequently used interchangeably with *nation branding*, *cultural relations* and *soft power*, causing even greater problems in communicating the precise meaning of cultural diplomacy (Melissen 2005). It is worth devoting some space in this chapter to the clarification of these overlapping terms and the drawing of boundaries around them. The following three sections define cultural diplomacy in relation to other concepts, pointing out existing similarities and differences between them.

Is museum diplomacy more than nation branding?

Cultural and museum diplomacy is frequently discussed in correlation to *nation branding*. It is a strategic form of international communication to "'sell' particular aspects of a nation to foreign publics" (Fitzpatrick 2010, 90). Nation branding usually deals with matters directly related to tourism, trade and investment. At the same time, it rests on spreading and popularising national ideals, values and identities employed to create a positive image of the country. Simon Anholt, the founder of the nation branding theory, explains that nation branding is primarily a marketing strategy. It draws on national myths and symbols to articulate aspirations for wealth, power and enhanced visibility (Anholt 2007). Nation branding aims to construct a favourable image of the country in the global context to improve its cultural, economic and political position on the world stage.

The main reason nation branding is frequently invoked in discussions of cultural diplomacy is simple. Promotional rhetoric and national projections have traditionally been used by governments in cultural diplomacy programs to elevate the popularity of national cultures and traditions internationally. For example, U.S. State Department cultural affairs diplomat Helena Finn has repeatedly emphasised in her public speeches that cultural diplomacy consists of "winning foreigners' voluntary allegiance to the American project" (Finn 2003, 16). American diplomacy scholar Nancy Snow has defined cultural diplomacy as "efforts to market a more positive image of America to the world" (Snow 2007, 209).

Furthermore, museums as "national expressions of identity" (Macdonald 2003, 3) have historically played a key role in promoting national ideologies and constituting citizenry (Bennett 1995; Karp 1991; Luke 2002; Pearce 1995). The strong power of museum objects to "stand for the nation" has been instrumental in the articulation of culture and national values on the global stage. Cold War examples of national promotion, facilitated by museums from both the U.S. and Soviet Russia, provide convincing evidence to this effect.

Another good example is a highly popular series of touring festivals; "Mexico: A Work of Art" was first hosted by the Metropolitan Museum in New York. It offered 150 museum exhibitions, performances and cultural events organised throughout the U.S. in the 1990s. The festival used Mexico as a means to promote national culture in the U.S. and internationally. "It is a time of change in Mexico, and in the relations between our two nations," Mexican Ambassador Jorge Alberto Lozoya stressed at the opening event. "We are not mysterious, or difficult to understand, and we want you to know that. We wanted to bring to New York the best of what we are" (Collins 1990). While promoting national history and the culture of Mexico, the festivals employed exoticising techniques "spectacularizing the nationalist myth" and circulating cultural treasures in a "blatant, self-admitted form of propaganda" (Wallis 1994, 279).

Indeed, both cultural and museum diplomacy have a promotional dimension. However, it would be too simplistic to equate it with nation branding. The latter one is a one-way or monological form of communication. It uses marketing principles to create and promote a rather simplified and one-dimensional image of a country in the eyes of the global public. Cultural diplomacy, in contrast, is based on an interactive dialogue and two-way flow of information that provides opportunities for people-to-people connections and engagements (Melissen 2005; Parkinson 1977). These contacts help participants learn about each other's differences and commonalities and negotiate common values in a matter that leads to mutual understanding, trust and respect (Parkinson 1977).

American historian Yale Richmond (2003) reviewed strategically designed educational, scientific, artistic and cultural exchanges implemented during the Cold War. He revealed that their strong effects in both societies were instrumental in exposing participants to real life on the other side. Cultural exchanges and museum programs encouraged participants' interest and curiosity in national traditions and customs while engaging human emotions, establishing strong human connections and generating a genuine interest and respect toward the other (Richmond 2003). As both Schneider (2006) and Goff (2013) point out, cultural diplomacy humanises international relations. While "official lines of communication can transmit a one-dimensional message," cultural diplomacy "complicates the official message or the prevailing image" through the development of a dialogue among participants (Goff 2013, 422).

Museum diplomacy requires strong collaborations among artists, curators, exhibition designers and other involved stakeholders. In this way, it overcomes stereotypical or simplistic projections of national culture (Goff 2013). While national governments support museum exchanges with a main goal of projecting a positive image abroad, the most powerful museum diplomacy does not happen on display (Anheier and Isar 2007). It exists behind the scenes when communities, artists and museum professionals come together to share their cultures and values (Grincheva 2015). Through these genuine human-to-human connections, museums can establish and maintain long-term cultural relations.

When cultural relations become museum diplomacy

While cultural diplomacy is shaped by the politics of geopolitical interest and foreign policy agenda, *cultural relations* "grow naturally and organically, without government intervention" (Arndt 2005). Both cultural relations and cultural diplomacy are predominantly based on people-to-people exchanges and connections. However, the main difference between them has been previously defined in terms of government involvement in funding and the design of international programs (Pamment 2012). As some scholars would argue, "much of what defines cultural relations (and what distinguishes it from cultural diplomacy) – the longer timescale, honesty, mutuality, and trust – is made possible by its independence from government" (Rivera 2015, 13).

Nevertheless, taking the government as a key variable in complex international relationships might not be the "most effective way of distinguishing between the practices of cultural diplomacy and cultural relations," as Rivera (2015) assumed (8). A top diplomacy scholar, Jan Melissen (2005), stressed that "it is neither helpful to hang on to past images of diplomacy [. . .] nor is it advisable to make a forward projection of historical practices into the present international environment" (16). In an era of increasing globalisation, it is important to acknowledge the complexities of challenging coexistence and interrelationships among state and non-state actors in the field of international relations (Hocking et al. 2012; Murray 2008). Within this perspective, cultural diplomacy exercised by non-state actors no longer fits a simplistic paradigm of diplomatic relations in which governments play the key role.

Moreover, as Melissen (2005) rightly pointed out, and as this book will further demonstrate, cultural institutions, including museums, prefer to keep the term "cultural relations for their own activities, serving the national interest indirectly by means of trust-building abroad" (21). These cultural relations significantly contribute to foreign policy objectives and "result in a measure of overlap with the work of diplomats" (22). While the power of non-state diplomacy is recognised in academic literature (Kelley 2014; Pamment 2012; Snow 2007), it remains unclear which international museum programs can be defined as a non-state form of cultural diplomacy and which are cultural relations.

In an age of increasing globalisation, the majority of large and middle-sized museums in growing metropolitan areas across countries are involved in cross-cultural activities in different capacities. For example, international museum blockbusters travel widely to different countries, bringing local and global audiences to museums. But it would be wrong to assume that all these international activities necessarily make museums cultural diplomats.

To draw boundaries between cultural diplomacy and cultural relations, it is useful to employ Ayhan's (2018) taxonomy of non-state actorness. Surveying a wide spectrum of public diplomacy scholarship, Ayhan identified five key criteria of non-state diplomacy. First, non-state actors of diplomacy must be institutionalised. Second, their activities must be based on communication with foreign publics. Third, they must have intentional diplomatic objectives, such as "understanding cultures, attitudes, and behaviour; building and managing relationships; and influencing opinions." Fourth, non-state actors must implement their international activities for collective interests rather than private interests. And, finally, their political goals must contribute to foreign policy objectives (Ayhan 2018, 11).

The majority of international museum engagements easily satisfy the first three requirements of non-state diplomacy. Museums are recognised institutionalised non-profit enterprises. Their international exhibitions and programs directly engage a wide constituency *in* foreign communities, including museum professionals, curators, artists, sponsors, media and audiences. Furthermore, as an important part of their missions and visions, the majority of museums intentionally commit to traditional objectives of diplomacy. Museums communicate values of cross-cultural understanding, trust and respect and aim to build long-term trustful relationships across borders. The mission of the Guggenheim, for example, is to

> preserve, and interpret modern and contemporary art, and explore ideas across cultures through dynamic curatorial and educational initiatives and collaborations. With its constellation of architecturally and culturally distinct museums, exhibitions, publications, and digital platforms, the foundation engages both local and global audiences.
>
> (Guggenheim 2018)

However, the final two criteria of non-state diplomacy, pursuing public versus private interests and contributing to the foreign policy agenda, seem to provide foundational principles to help differentiate between museum diplomacy and cultural relations. For example, the Guggenheim's bold developments in global corporatisation and museum franchising are less transparent and require more in-depth exploration. But some other cases of global expansion practices, such as Louvre Abu Dhabi, stand out as excellent examples of cultural diplomacy with a straightforward foreign policy agenda on the part of both involved stakeholders (Goff 2017).

Opened in 2017, Louvre Abu Dhabi is a direct collaboration between the French and Abu Dhabi governments that combines "the UAE's bold vision of cultural progression and openness with Frances's expertise in the world of art and museums" (Abu Dhabi Tourism & Culture Authority 2017). While directly serving the French government's cultural diplomacy goals, expanding its geopolitical military presence and interests in the region (McAuley 2017), the new Louvre museum creates a unique ideological and diplomatic space. In this space, national projections of the French empire collide with Abu Dhabi's global aspirations of rebranding the city as a top world cultural destination to facilitate "multicultural exchange between local, regional and international art landscapes" (Abu Dhabi Tourism & Culture Authority 2017).

Not only does Louvre Abu Dhabi demonstrate that museum franchising can be successfully used as a dedicated channel of official cultural diplomacy but, more importantly, it also illustrates that internationally recognised museums such as the Louvre have developed powerful brands, reputations and expertise on the global stage that generate soft power and the power to mobilise global audiences, attract international investments and develop bridges of cross-cultural collaboration.

Museums as centres of soft power

Cultural diplomacy as a tool for cultural influence is frequently conceptualised through the notion of *soft power*, coined and developed by Joseph Nye (2004). Cultural diplomacy resides on the soft power side of the hard power–soft power equation (Goff 2013, 420). The reason soft power is a suitable framework for cultural diplomacy activities is because, according to Nye (2004), culture constitutes one of the country's most important resources for the projection of soft power. A country possesses soft power if it is capable of exploiting the power of culture and ideas to shape and inhabit the mind space of another country through attraction rather than coercion (Nye 2004).

In order to generate soft power, cultural resources or assets need to be activated through a set of specific initiatives that reach foreign audiences to achieve a target response (Nye 2011). For example, Nye specifically favoured American pop culture as one of the greatest assets of U.S. soft power. American pop culture as a resource is activated by transnational media and entertainment corporations that circulate American values, ideals and symbols around the globe without any intention of exercising cultural diplomacy. However, as Nye (2004) stressed, Hollywood film industries succeeded in making "the United States seem to others exciting, exotic, rich, powerful, trend-setting and the cutting edge of modernity and innovation" (12).

Cultural diplomacy offers another pathway through which cultural resources can be activated to target international audiences and generate soft power. In relation to museums, governments used to play the key role in activating museum collections to travel abroad and create opportunities for cross-cultural exchange and engagements. This book, though, offers to explore museum franchising and global corporatisation as new and powerful ways to wield soft power, while redefining museum diplomacy in the twenty-first century. It argues that museum branches in foreign lands, as well as international projects supported by museums' self-revenue or implemented on the expense of corporate partners, can generate soft power, positioning museums as key actors of diplomacy.

Originally meant to explain the behaviour of nation states, the concept of soft power has recently acquired a much wider use. Employing the concept of soft power, organisational scholars identified a new form of influence exerted by a growing body of institutions operating across borders. This institutional soft power could be defined as

> a form of influence, persuasion, and identification, whereby stakeholders, stake seekers, and key publics are convinced to join or become a

> part of a group, organization, or cause [. . .] because they believe in an organization and/or its leaders.
>
> (Kenta et al. 2016, 95)

Organisational power of attraction is a meaningful way to extend soft power theory, exactly because Nye (2004) himself attributed it to more than state actors alone. Instead, he stressed the significance of civil society and non-state actors in taking the lead in projecting the power of attraction on the world stage.

It does not come as a surprise to see how contemporary museums employ soft power rhetoric to claim their contributions to building bridges of cross-cultural collaborations and attracting international investments and tourism (Lord and Blankenberg 2015). For example, Tristram Hunt, Director of the Victoria and Albert Museum, has pointed out that the museum's cultural resources and international engagements generate soft power. Its touring exhibitions, reaching millions of visitors in dozens of countries, and partnerships across cultural institutions and civil society at home and abroad "provide an innovative, and often revolutionary, sense of what contemporary British culture and identity can offer" (Hunt 2018).

Lord and Blankenberg (2015) made this argument particularly evocative in their book *Museums, Cities and Soft Power*. Their publication aimed to demonstrate that in the twenty-first century, museums are gradually transforming from "sites of branded experience to places of soft power" (13). Drawing on multiple case studies from different countries, including India, China, Brazil, Egypt and others, the authors argue that museums become key centres of soft power in a growing competition among cities for talent, tourism and investment. Considering the edited collection was written by museum professionals and consultants, rather than academics, these claims still need a more rigorous and critical appraisal in academia.

The present book offers a more nuanced exploration of museum soft power and relates it to contemporary forms of cultural diplomacy. It positions contemporary museums as active actors on the world stage that can generate the power of attractiveness, especially in cases in which state actors suffer from a lack of credibility on the global stage. The case studies from Russia and China, as authoritarian regimes, specifically illuminate how contemporary museums from less democratic societies take on important roles and carry out diplomatic missions without necessarily relying on support from their national governments. In this way, the book documents the development of new forms of cultural diplomacy based on the Guggenheim's models of global expansion.

Conclusion: defining non-state museum diplomacy

This chapter discussed two important components of non-state museum diplomacy. First, focusing on non-state legitimacy, it defined a non-state actor of cultural diplomacy as a non-governmental organisation that is able to exercise powerful social or cultural influence at national and international levels. Such an organisation gains its legitimacy through three important diplomatic capabilities. These are: (1) constant development of a global expertise or reputation; (2) nurturing credibility through autonomously standing outside the direct control of a national government; and (3) an institutional capacity to generate funding in support of its global activities through effective resources and alliance building.

A museum can acquire diplomatic legitimacy as a non-state player of cultural diplomacy if it is an internationally recognised institution with a strong global reputation. This museum should also have a credible image in the eyes of global audiences by keeping its international activities and programs outside government control. Finally, in order to keep its independence from political influence, a museum should find ways to economically support its international programs through different private and corporate sources or self-earned revenue.

Defining cultural diplomacy in relation to national branding, cultural relations and soft power, the chapter identified several important criteria that delineate the boundaries of museum diplomacy. In contrast to nation branding, museum diplomacy is based on people-to-people exchanges and collaborations that bring participants together for an interactive dialogue. However, these museum international exchanges and cultural relations across countries can only transform into cultural diplomacy if they meet certain requirements of non-state actors (Ayhan 2018). To be recognised as players of diplomacy, museums have to serve public interests rather than pursue their own strategic development goals or the objectives of their patrons on the global stage. Furthermore, a museum's international activities must meaningfully contribute to, or complement, the foreign policy objectives of their national states, while being self-initiated rather than facilitated by state incentives.

Finally, museums become powerful non-state actors of cultural diplomacy when they are able to project their own soft power. This museum soft power draws on institutional capacities to effectively employ its cultural resources to reach out and mobilise audiences, build international bridges of collaboration across countries and attract a wide constituency to support cultural causes of diplomatic significance. The following two chapters offer examples of non-state museum diplomacy, particularly in the cases of the State Hermitage Museum in Russia and K11 Art Mall from China. These cases are evidence that in the twenty-first century, museum franchising and global corporatisation have established themselves in the museum world as alternative ways to exercise cultural diplomacy.

References

Abu Dhabi Tourism & Culture Authority (ADT&CA). 2017. Museums. http://tcaabudhabi.ae/en/what.we.do/culture/museums.aspx (accessed July 2017).

Anheier, Helmut and Yudhishthir Isar. 2007. *Cultures and Globalization: Conflicts and Tensions*. The Cultures and Globalization Series. Thousand Oaks, CA: Sage Publications.

Anholt, Simon. 2007. *Competitive Identity: The New Brand Management for Nations, Cities and Regions*. New York, NY: Palgrave Macmillan.

Arndt, Richard. 2005. *First Resort of Kings: American Cultural Diplomacy in the 20th Century*. Washington, DC: Potomac Books.

Avant, Deborah, Finnemore, Martha and Susan Sell. 2010. *Who Governs the Globe?* Cambridge: Cambridge University Press.

Ayhan, Kadir. 2018. The Boundaries of Public Diplomacy and Nonstate Actors: A Taxonomy of Perspectives. *International Studies Perspectives* 10: 1–21.

Barnett, Michael and Martha Finnemore. 2005. The Power of Liberal International Organizations. In *Power in Global Governance*, eds. Michael Barnett and Raymond Duvall. Cambridge: Cambridge University Press.

Bennett, Tony. 1995. *The Birth of the Museum: History, Theory, Politics*. London: Routledge.

Binns, Gareth. 2005. The Universal Museum. Institute of Historical Research. https://core.ac.uk/download/pdf/9047001.pdf (accessed December 2018).

Blair, Elizabeth and Steve Inskeep. 2007. Museum Connect. National Public Radio. www.npr.org (accessed October 2012).

Collins, Glenn. 1990. From Mexico, Dance, Theater, Music and 30 Centuries of Art. *New York Times*, 11 September.

Cummings, Milton. 2003. *Cultural Diplomacy and the United States Government: A Survey*. Cultural Diplomacy Research Series. Washington, DC: Americans for the Arts.

Dilevko, Juris and Lisa Gottlieb. 2004. *The Evolution of Library and Museum Partnerships: Historical Antecedents, Contemporary Manifestations, and Future Directions*. Westport, CT: Libraries Unlimited.

Duncan, Carol. 1995. *Civilizing Rituals: Inside Public Art Museums*. Routledge.

Edwards, Michael. 1999. International Development NGOs: Agents of Foreign Aid or Vehicles of International Cooperation? *Non-Profit and Voluntary Sector Quarterly* 28: 25–37.

Finn, HelenaK. 2003. The Case for Cultural Diplomacy. *Foreign Affairs* 82(6): 15–20.

Fitzpatrick, Kathy. 2010. *The Future of U.S. Public Diplomacy: An Uncertain Fate*. Boston, MA: Brill.

Goff, Patricia. 2013. Cultural Diplomacy. In *The Oxford Handbook of Modern Diplomacy*, eds. Andrew Cooper, Jorge Heine and Ramesh Thakur. Oxford: Oxford University Press.

Goff, Patricia. 2017. The Museum as a Transnational Actor. *Arts and International Affairs* 2(1).

Gilboa, Eytan. 2008. Searching for a Theory of Public Diplomacy. *The ANNALS of the American Academy of Political and Social Science* 616(1): 55–77.

Grincheva, Natalia. 2015. Democracy for Export: Museums Connect Program as a Vehicle of American Cultural Diplomacy. *Curator, the Museum Journal* 58(2): 137–149.

Guggenheim. 2018. About Us. www.guggenheim.org/about-us (accessed July 2018).

Guilbaut, Serge. 2005. Sleeping in Bilbao: The Guggenheim as a New Cultural Edsel? In *Learning from the Guggenheim Bilbao*, eds. Anna Maria Guasch and Joseba Zulaika, 133–147. Reno: Center for Basque Studies, University of Nevada.

Hocking, Brian, Melissen, Jan, Riordan, Shaun and Paul Sharp. 2012. *Integrative Diplomacy in the 21st Century*. The Hague: Netherlands Institute of International Relations.

Hoggard, Liz. 2006. Our National Treasurer. *Guardian*, 26 March.

Hunt, Tristram. 2018. The Transformational (Soft) Power of Museums: At Home and Abroad. Center of Public Diplomacy. https://bit.ly/2FNRxye (accessed October 2018).

Jenkins, Tiffany. 2009. Artists, Resist This Propagandist Agenda. *Spicked*, 27 October.

Johnson, Georgie. 2016. BP Pursues Egyptian Oil Deals Whilst Sponsoring Blockbuster Egypt Exhibition at British Museum. *Energy Desk Green Piece*, May.

Jora, Lucian. 2013. New Practices and Trends in Cultural Diplomacy. *Political Science and International Relations* 10(1): 43–52.

Karp, Ivan. 1991. Cultures in Museums Perspectives. In *Exhibiting Cultures: The Poetics and Politics of Museum Display*, ed. Ivan Karp. Washington, DC: Smithsonian Institution Press.

Kelley, John. 2010. The New Diplomacy: Evolution of a Revolution. *Diplomacy & Statecraft* 21: 286–305.

Kelley, John. 2014. *Agency Change*. London: Rowman & Littlefield.

Kenta, Michael, Sommerfeldtb, Erich J. and Adam J. Saffer. 2016. Social Networks, Power, and Public Relations: Tertius Iungens as a Cocreational Approach to Studying Relationship Networks. *Public Relations Review* 42(1): 91–100.

Kleiner, Juergen. 2008. The Inertia of Diplomacy, Diplomacy & Statecraft. *Diplomacy & Statecraft* 19(2): 321–349.

La Porte, Teresa. 2012. The Legitimacy and Effectiveness of Non-State Actors and the Public Diplomacy Concept. In *Public Diplomacy Theory and Conceptual Issues*, International Studies Association, ISA Annual Convention, San Diego.

Lord, Gail and Ngaire Blankenberg. 2015. *Museums, Cities and Soft Power*. Washington, DC: American Association of Museums.

Luke, Timothy. 2002. *Museum Politics: Power Plays at the Exhibition*. Minneapolis, MN: University of Minnesota Press.

Macdonald, Sharon. 2003. Museums, National, Postnational and Transcultural Identities. *Museum and Society* 1(1): 1–16.

MacGregor, Neil. 2012. To Shape the Citizens of "That Great City, the World." In *Whose Culture? The Promise of Museums and the Debate Over Antiquities*, ed. James Cuno, 39–54. Princeton, NJ: Princeton University Press.

McAuley, James. 2017. Soft Power: The Louvre Starts a Lucrative New Chapter in Abu Dhabi. *The Sydney Morning Herald*, 9 November.

Melissen, Jan. 2005. *The New Public Diplomacy: Soft Power in International Relations*. New York, NY: Palgrave Macmillan.

Melissen, Jan. 2006. *The New Public Diplomacy: Between Theory and Practice.* London,UK: Palgrave Macmillan.

Miller, Toby. 2014. Global arts scene awash with big oil and gas sponsorship. *The Conversations*, April 14.

Mitchell, George. 2014. Strategic Responses to Resource Dependence Among Transnational NGOs Registered in the United States. *Voluntas* 25: 67–91.

Murray, Stuart. 2008. Consolidating the Gains Made in Diplomacy Studies: A Taxonomy. *International Studies Perspectives* 9(1): 22–39.

Nye, Joseph. 2004. *Soft Power: The Means to Success in World Politics.* New York, NY: Public Affairs.

Nye, Joseph. 2011. *The Future of Power.* New York, NY: Perseus Group.

Pamment, James. 2012. *New Public Diplomacy in the 21st Century a Comparative Study of Policy and Practice.* New York, NY: Routledge.

Parkinson, F. 1977. *The Philosophy of International Relations: A Study in the History of Thought.* Beverly Hills, CA: Sage Publications.

Pearce, Susan. 1995. *Art in Museums*. Continuum International Publishing Group.

Potter, Evan. 2002. *Cyber-Diplomacy: Managing Foreign Policy in the Twenty-First Century.* Montreal: McGill-Queen's Press.

Reinalda, Bob and Bertjan Verbeek. 2001. Theorizing Power Relations Between NGOs, Intergovernmental Organizations and States. In *Non-State Actors in International Relations*, eds. Bas Arts, Math Noortmann and Bob Reinalda, 145–158. Farnham: Ashgate.

Richmond, Yale. 2003. *Cultural Exchange and the Cold War: Raising the Iron Curtain.* University Park, PA: Penn State University Press.

Rivera, Tim. 2015. *Distinguishing Cultural Relations from Cultural Diplomacy: The British Council's Relationship with Her Majesty's Government.* Los Angeles, CA: Figueroa Press.

Rosenbaum, Lee. 2007. AAM Collaborates in U.S. Program Co-opting Museums as Agents of Foreign Policy. *Arts Journal.* www.artsjournal.com/culture grrl/2007/07/aam_collaborates_in_us_program.html (accessed July 2017).

Rubin Museum of Art (RMA). 2004. The World Is Sound. www.artsy.net/rubin museum/overview (accessed July 2017).

Schneider, Cynthia. 2003. *Diplomacy That Works: Best Practices in Cultural Diplomacy.* Washington DC: Georgetown University: Center for Arts and Culture.

Schneider, Cynthia. 2006. Culture Communicates: US Diplomacy That Works. In *The New Public Diplomacy*, eds. Jan Melissen, Donna Lee and Paul Sharp. New York, NY: Palgrave Macmillan.

Science Gallery International. 2018. About Us. https://international.sciencegallery.com/international (accessed July 2018).

Scott-Smith, Giles. 2009. Exchange Programs and Public Diplomacy. In *Routledge Handbook of Public Diplomacy*, eds. Nancy Snow and Philip Taylor, 50–56. New York, NY: Routledge.

Snow, Nancy. 2007. *The Arrogance of American Power: What U.S. Leaders Are Doing Wrong and Why It's Our Duty to Dissent*. Lanham, MD: Rowman & Littlefield.

Snow, Nancy and Philip Taylor. 2009. *Routledge Handbook of Public Diplomacy*. New York, NY: Routledge.

Spiro, Peter. 2013. Constraining Global Corporate Power: A Short Introduction. *Vanderbilt Journal of Transnational Law* 46: 1101–1118.

Telegraph. 2011. Donny George. 11 March.

U.S. Department of State. 1969. Cultural Diplomacy. International Education Exchange Service, Washington DC: US Department of State Bureau of International Cultural Relations.

U.S. Department of State. 2012. Museums Connect. www.benefits.gov/benefit/5915 (accessed July 2018).

U.S. Department of State Archive. 2005. President and Secretary Honor Ambassador Karen Hughes at Swearing-in Ceremony. 9 September. https://bit.ly/2PaEWVj (accessed July 2018).

Vezirgiannidou, Sevasti-Eleni. 2013. The United States and Rising Powers in a Post-Hegemonic Global Order. *International Affairs* 89(3): 635–651.

Wallis, Brian. 1994. Selling Nations: International Exhibitions and Cultural Diplomacy. In *Globalization: Specialized Applications and Resistance to Globalization*, eds. Roland Robertson and Kathleen White, 177–191. Minneapolis, MN: University of Minnesota Press.

2 Museum diplomacy as a corporate enterprise

Gone are the times that museums could rely solely on their national governments to organise cultural exchanges or take their collections on international tours. What was previously a highly political matter with a strategic geopolitical focus and concern is now an economic necessity for many museums around the world. Reflecting on the expansion of museum shops, the rise of blockbuster exhibitions and a global proliferation of corporate sponsorships, McClellan (2008) has pointed out that "perhaps, no development in the art museum of the last half-century has been more dramatic or controversial than the increase in commercialism" (221).

Contemporary museums have become more sensitive and responsive to global art market demands, new management trends and financial models of operation in transnational economic environments (Vivant 2011, 101). They adopt global corporatisation strategies, as their survival directly depends "on their ability to compete locally, nationally, and globally, for sponsorship and also for audiences" (Fraser 2006, 150). The new museology is a result of the "convergence of museums, the heritage industry and tourism, profit-making and pleasure-giving" (McLaughlin 1997). Not only is this convergence grounded in expanding partnerships and collaborations with transnational corporations, but museums also compete for global visitors by developing corporate infrastructures that offer more shopping, dining and entertainment.

Andy Warhol once remarked that "all department stores will become museums and all museums will become department stores" (Gomez 2002, 43). In the twenty-first century, this prophecy has become a reality with the phenomenon of K11 Art Mall, the first retail-based museum in the world, which emerged beyond the Western hemisphere. K11 Art Mall was opened by Adrian Cheng, a member of the third richest family in Hong Kong, owners of the New World, Chow Tai Fook property and a jewellery empire. K11 brings "a curated art and culture experience into a retail space" (Cheng 2018). "You can't separate the two [museum and shopping mall] with K11," the founder explained. "Everything you see inside a K11 Art Mall is to create a sense of wonder just like when you step inside a museum" (Cheng 2018).

The emergence of the retail-based museum is not surprising. Museums have been steadily commercialising their practices for decades, with the first successful examples of this trend emerging in the nineteenth century (McClellan 2008). However, as many museum critics would agree, no museum has gone further to emulate a business model than the Guggenheim under Thomas Krens. He is "the venture capitalist of the museum world, leveraging the Guggenheim collection and exporting the Guggenheim brand to new 'branch' museums around the world" (McClellan 2008, 221).

With Krens's arrival at the Guggenheim in the late twentieth century, the world of museums acquired a whole new vocabulary in describing museums in terms of museum industry, capitalisation, mergers and acquisitions, as well as asset management and products (Krauss 1990, 17). Since the 1990s, Krens has openly embraced corporate practices "by hosting exhibitions of motorcycles, Armani fashion, and the paintings of Norman Rockwell and doing business with a Las Vegas casino" (McClellan 2008, 221).

The Guggenheim and K11 are both the focus of this chapter, which aims to investigate the convergence between museums and corporations by interrogating its implications for contemporary museum diplomacy. While the first sections will explore the development of the global corporatisation model in the context of the Guggenheim, the following part will analyse this practice in its further transformations and adaptations among a new generation of Chinese museums. It will focus on K11 as a unique case that is particularly representative of the global convergence between the corporate world and contemporary museums.

The chapter offers provocative illustrations of how museums employ global corporatisation to support their activities on the international stage. These examples expose how museums and national governments, in the context of rapidly growing neo-liberal globalisation, redefine their roles and responsibilities. These changes give birth to a new form of museum diplomacy. It is established as a corporate enterprise with a distinct social mission, rather than as an ideologically driven initiative commissioned by a national government. But let us start at the very beginning, with the development of the corporate Guggenheim.

The corporate Guggenheim: Krensian economics of museum success

The Guggenheim Museum has an interesting history. It was established by a successful American family, the Guggenheim brothers, who immigrated from Switzerland and Germany around 1848 – and in a short time managed to develop a thriving mining business. Guggenheim and Sons was the corporate crown of a classic American success story: "Meyer Guggenheim, the son of an immigrant Swiss tailor, had grown from modest beginnings as a street peddler to accumulate a small fortune in the wholesale goods and lace trades" (O'Brien 1989, 124). Starting in Colorado, the family soon opened mining companies in Mexico, Alaska and Chile. With the growth of their wealth, two of the brothers, Benjamin and Solomon Guggenheim, started to collect modern art (Davis 1994).

Solomon toured Europe to visit artists' studios and purchase their works, which eventually formed one of the largest collections of modern paintings by artists such as Vasily Kandinsky, Paul Klee, Marc Chagall and others (Davis 1994). In 1937, the Solomon R. Guggenheim Foundation was established as a private "educational corporation for the mental or moral improvement of men and women, the promotion and encouragement of art and education" (Vail 2009, 25). The collection was first exhibited in the small Art of This Century Gallery on East 54th Street in New York. In 1959, it was moved to a new building designed by Frank Lloyd Wright, a landmark work of twentieth century architecture that, to this day, attracts a great number of visitors and tourists impressed by the museum's design.

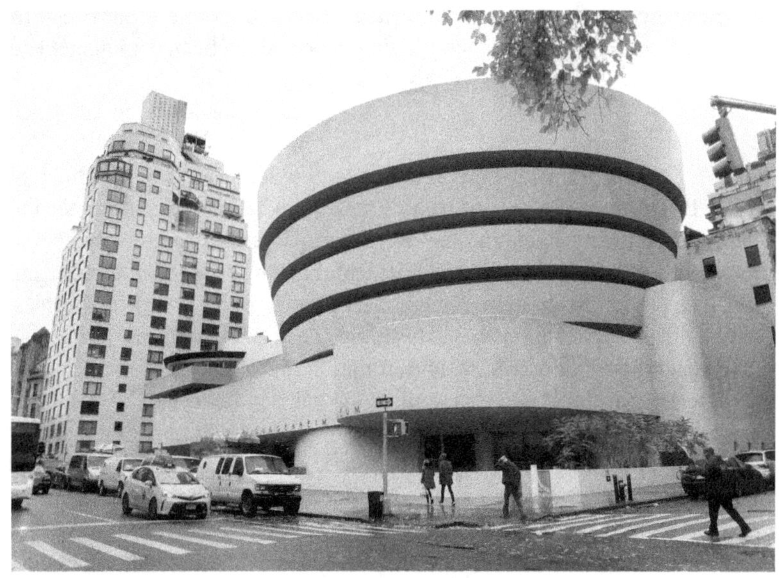

Figure 2.1 Guggenheim Museum, New York (USA)

Source: Photograph by Natalia Grincheva, November 2018.

The Guggenheim's corporate development is usually associated with such figures as Thomas Krens, the Guggenheim's director from 1988 to 2008. He arrived in the museum with an "MBA from Yale instead of the required doctorate in Art History" (Mathur 2005, 698) and started his career with a scandal and a deal worth $47 million for selling Chagall, Kandinsky and Modigliani from the Guggenheim's permanent collection (Kimmelman 1999). Even though Krens's bold leadership transformed the museum and almost sextupled the investment in the foundation from $20 million to $118 million (Fabelová 2010, 53), his contribution was an effect rather than a cause.

The corporate Guggenheim is a result of the museum's strategic governance and leadership. Peter Lawson-Johnston, who has served on the Board of Trustees as Chair since 1970 – for more than 40 years – honestly acknowledged his involvement in the corporate development of the museum in the late twentieth century. "I am neither a collector nor a particularly astute judge of art," he said, adding:

> People are frequently surprised that my contributions to the Guggenheim are those of a business manager. [. . .] The international language of art institutions is also the language of business: stewardship, management, acquisition, showmanship, and solvency. [. . .] Business and museums can learn much from each other, and more museums can be run more efficiently by employing more sophisticated management practices.
>
> (Lawson-Johnston 2014, 13)

In 1969, Lawson-Johnston inherited the position of president of the Guggenheim's Board from his cousin, Harry Frank, who had never felt the need to seek funding from outside the family. Lawson-Johnston completely altered the course of the Foundation's development. First, he changed its status from private to public. Second, he brought new people to the Board of Trustees. Specifically, Lawson-Johnston focused on those who could do more than make generous annual contributions or long-term capital gift commitments. He aimed to build a Board that could encourage and oversee the corporate development of the museum. During his presidency, he appointed many owners of large corporations to the Board. Some of these appointments included Morgan Bank Chair and World Bank Director Lew Preston; Gould Corporation Chair Bill Ylvisaker; Mobile Chairman and CEO Rawleigh Warner; Kennecott Copper President Frank Milliken; and many other successful and wealthy American businessmen (Lawson-Johnston 2014, 137).

The real secret of the Guggenheim's achievements in the world of art, as Lawson-Johnston (2014) used to say, "is that [. . .] few of the Guggenheims [. . .] have themselves been deeply informed collectors or curators"; rather, they had strong "business acumen" and talents "responsible for success of the entire enterprise" (10). Among his major appointments at the managerial level, Thomas Krens was the key person who understood perfectly the corporate spirit of the foundation. "Art institutions are not really different from other businesses," Krens stressed, "at least not when they act like them" (Kimmelman 2002). In his memoir, Lawson-Johnston (2014) distinguished Krens as one of the most important figures in the history of the Guggenheim. With special sympathy, gratitude and admiration, he wrote that Krens had been "the principle force behind the museum's ascension to an enterprise of truly global dimension" (Lawson-Johnston 2014, 15).

Krens was not only the leader of the first museum franchise in the world but also consistently integrated corporate logic into museum management and operations on multiple levels. He believed "that the historic model of the museum was on the edge of obsolescence" (Trilupaityte 2009, 125). His formula for museum success consisted of the following important elements: "great collections, great architecture, a great special exhibition, a great second exhibition, two shopping opportunities, two eating opportunities, a high-tech interface via the Internet, and economies of scale via a global network" (Cuno 2001, 45).

In terms of collections and architecture, Krens's strategies were focused on strengthening the most important museum assets the Guggenheim already had. The museum building facilities, and even its collections and artworks, according to Krens, should be successfully employed for the development of an experience-centred museum. A contemporary museum, as he believed, should "forego history in the name of a kind of intensity of experience, an aesthetic charge that is not so much temporal (historical) as it is now radically spatial" (Krauss 1990, 7).

Understanding that the spiral museum architecture has always been "a magnet for crowds," Krens was able to turn the Guggenheim building into a space of public consumption (Conn 2010). In fact, far more postcards are sold of the building than paintings on display (Watkin 1991), while as many as a third of the Guggenheim's visitors come to see the architecture rather than the exhibitions or permanent collections on view (Guggenheim 2013). Building on this strong appeal, Krens maximised the experience-centred management approach by employing museum spaces as key generators of self-earned revenue.

Not only did these strategies include expanding shopping and dining opportunities, they also offered new public programs for leisure and entertainment, including film screenings, receptions, cocktail parties and celebrations. A high turnout of visitors generated an equally high economic return. Furthermore, renting out museum spaces and curating "site-specific commissions rather than traditional collections" (Krauss 1990, 7) significantly strengthened economic sustainability and the Guggenheim's autonomy.

Not surprisingly, as reflected in IRS 990 tax reports from 2001 to 2012, Program Service Revenue, as a part of the Guggenheim's annual income, significantly exceeded the amount of support received from other sources. Program Service Revenue includes admission fees, special events income, restaurant and retail store sales, fees for museum special services and unrelated business income. It constitutes, on average, $27 million each year, or more than 45 per cent of the Guggenheim's total annual budget. In comparison, the Metropolitan Museum of Art in New York generates only 3 per cent through its Program Service Revenue, relying more on philanthropic support, grants, donations and pledges from its patrons (Metropolitan Museum 2011–2015).

Combined with annual membership dues, the Guggenheim's annual self-earned income makes half of its $60 million budget. The other half also has a corporate nature. Sponsorship from transnational corporations, through gifts and pledges, contributes around $23.5 million annually. Under Krens, the museum developed a strong tradition of partnerships with wealthy corporate patrons, from not only the U.S. but also across the globe.

For example, since 1996 the museum has enjoyed corporate support from Hugo Boss, a global luxury fashion and style company of German origin. It provides substantial financial assistance to tour several exhibitions each year (Rectanus 2002). "Hugo Boss is one of our most important and long-standing corporate patrons," the Chairman of the Guggenheim's Board of Trustees said. "In addition to funding several exhibitions, they also completely fund the biennial Hugo Boss Prize – a major, juried contemporary art invitational whose winner receives $50,000 and a show at the Guggenheim" (Lawson-Johnston 2014, 136).

One of Krens's "more ingenious initiatives" has been the Global Partners program, in which corporations receive prominent recognition in all of the Guggenheim's venues in return for making generous donations to the Foundation. "Rather than sponsor an exhibit confined to a single museum, these Global Partners enjoy continual recognition in all Guggenheim museums over months or even years" (Lawson-Johnston 2014, 137). Delta Airlines, for example, is one of the most active Global Partners. It provides donations-in-kind, such as gratis flights for museum personnel and artwork shipments, as well as sponsorship of travelling exhibitions that benefit from the Guggenheim's presence and visibility in North America and Europe (Lawson-Johnston 2014, 137).

The Global Partners program has allowed the museum to tap into international resources and stretch its corporate investments beyond U.S. borders. However, Krens multiplied the income from corporate sponsorship when he started to produce highly successful but controversial blockbuster exhibitions in collaboration with large transnational corporations. These exhibits brought the Guggenheim to a new level of global outreach and visibility while maximising economic return.

One of the first corporate blockbusters was the famous 1998 show "Art of the Motorcycle," known as the Guggenheim Museum's landmark exhibition. Designed by Frank O. Gehry and generously sponsored by the German car company BMW, it presented the evolution and design of motorcycle technology. The exhibit showcased more than 130 motorcycles arranged chronologically, beginning with the 1868 Michaux Perreaux (Guggenheim 2001). It turned out to be highly popular among the general public, drawing more than 4,000 visitors a day and more than 5,000 people on weekends (Vogel 1998).

Overall, the attendance in New York was 301,037 – one of the largest in the history of the Guggenheim (Sheller and Urry 2004). For many of the show attendees, it was the first museum visit of their lives (Packer 2008, 112). Even though the show turned the museum into a "parking lot," it brought larger and more diverse audiences to experience a new kind of museum, one that strongly appealed to the public's taste. With financial support from BMW, the "Art of the Motorcycle" travelled for three years to different museums in the U.S. and abroad, "drawing huge crowds at every stop" (Rogers et al. 2003, 252). For example, attendance at the Guggenheim Bilbao was overall around 3 million. In Las Vegas at the opening night of the Guggenheim–Hermitage satellite, attendance reached more than 250,000 (Sheller and Urry 2004).

Another controversial but popular among the masses exhibition was curated by Giorgio Armani, the world-famous Italian designer. He pledged $15 million to the museum, entering into a long-term relationship with the foundation (Potvin 2012, 48). The exhibit "Giorgio Armani" featured 400 garments and offered a thematic look at Armani's fashion design over the previous 25 years. It set new attendance records for the Guggenheim, bringing more than 4,000 visitors a day to see the show. In total, 283,000 people viewed the exhibit in New York (Sheller and Urry 2004). The popular extravaganza later travelled to the Guggenheim Bilbao and other venues around Europe, attracting large audiences and interest among the general public (Haacke 2012).

The new model of museum exhibitions based on "soliciting corporations – like BMW, Giorgio Armani, or Hugo Boss – to sponsor 'shows' of their own products" was severely criticised. Both in academia and in the museum world, Krens was blamed for turning the Guggenheim into a modern boutique or place of consumption (Sorkin 2005, 25). For example, Loughery (2001) described the Guggenheim's shift from serious artistic scholarship to sensational programming in the following way:

> The Guggenheim deserves credit for some important exhibitions in the last decade . . . This is the museum where we have studied Kandinsky and the Russian avant-garde in the greatest detail possible in America . . . But this is also an institution that seems most proud of its 1998

> motorcycle survey, largely because that show brought in unprecedented revenues from visitors who have no interest in Kandinsky or Picasso.
> (632)

By associating itself with the names of big corporations, the Guggenheim "links its image to a post-modernism of visual consumption, that is, of contemporary fashion, irony, and a cosmopolitan life style" (Rectanus 2002, 187). These commercially driven partnerships shape a populist and consumerist logic of museum programming concerned with generating large audiences and bringing higher profits. Reflecting on its collaborations with commercial brands, the Guggenheim sponsorship director shared the following:

> Guggenheim is a corporate-friendly environment for sponsorship but at times it has been seen as too corporate-oriented and perceived as if corporations are coming in and determining the programming. But it is really not that at all. It is much more of a collaboration and the programming is always handled 100% by Guggenheim.
> (Lund and Greyser 2015, 11)

Whether or not the museum has full control of its artistic programming while embarking on collaborations with transnational patrons, the Guggenheim demonstrates a strong capacity to attract global publics and generate profitable revenue. "The issue isn't about the number of buildings or exhibitions," Krens once remarked, "but the number of people you directly engage with" (Trilupaityte 2009, 126). Partnerships with transnational corporations push the Guggenheim to be experimental and to employ responsible populist logic for making its programming a global success. The museum operates on the strong emotional engagement of masses, through either non-traditional offerings and unique spatial experiences or inclusive participative opportunities designed not necessarily for art lovers but mostly for general publics.

Both the visitors' admiration for, and appreciation of, the museum, as well as a high remuneration from corporate sponsors, show that Krensian economics work well to strengthen the museum's economic sustainability. It has also increased its global audiences and improved its brand recognition in different parts of the world. Continuing this legacy, in recent years the scope and reach of the global Guggenheim programs significantly increased, reflecting the growing appetites of corporate partners to enter new geographic markets. Two examples that illustrate this trend among more recent corporate engagement with transnational corporations are a collaboration with Google on the YouTube Play project (2010) and a partnership with the global financial services company UBS on the MAP

Global Art Initiative (2012–2017). Both are excellent illustrations of the Guggenheim's continuous global corporatisation agenda, which is based on its institutional ambition to open up the museum "to think globally and act globally" and to completely redefine "what 'international' means in the 21st century" (Havis 2015).

For example, in collaboration with Google, the largest transnational media company, YouTube Play was designed as an international contest of creative videos. It aimed to engage global YouTubers, emerging digital artists and amateur filmmakers from around the world. The contest generated 23,358 online video submissions from 91 countries, "which is unheard of in a traditional art context" (Hughes 2010). Around 125 shortlisted videos featured on the YouTube Play channel garnered more than 10 million online viewers the day of the live celebration event at the Guggenheim. This number of views exceeded the number of total annual online visits to the Guggenheim website in 2010. More than a year after completion of the project, YouTube Play still attracted over 23 million viewers from all over the world. To date, it remains one of the most popular YouTube channels, with around 65,000 subscribers and millions of followers posting on the channel in 26 languages.

However, "one of the most far-reaching curatorial, educational research projects that the Guggenheim museum has ever undertaken" was the five-year UBS MAP Global Art Initiative. It was also "the most ambitious philanthropic partnerships that the UBS has ever sponsored" (Munroe 2012). UBS invested $40 million in the project to support a network of art, artists and curators from South and South-East Asia, Latin America, the Middle East and North Africa. The project offered a program of curatorial residencies, international touring exhibitions and educational activities to challenge the "Western-centric view of art history" by expanding the Guggenheim's collections and programming to new geographic areas of developing countries (Vogel 2012). On completion of the project, Guggenheim acquired more than one hundred new contemporary artworks from under-represented regions in the global art world. Touring shows and curatorial residencies engaged one hundred emerging artists from different countries. The project established links and connections among local communities across five continents, bringing new voices and ideas from Africa, Latin America, the Middle East and Asia (Guggenheim 2001).

With such international reach and visibility, and the strong power to attract global attention, the Guggenheim is well placed to project U.S. soft power and exercise cultural diplomacy. Arguably, numerous travelling exhibitions, artistic residencies, exchange and educational events in different parts of the world establish a robust platform for productive cross-cultural dialogue that paves the way for cultural diplomacy. But has this ever been the museum's concern or commitment? Famous American art critic and journalist Deborah Solomon once pointed out that the Guggenheim is "a model of frankness and American pragmatism . . . It does not pretend that art is religion or that the museum is church" (Sylvester 2009, 119). While embracing the growing forces of neo-liberal globalisation in pursuit of its own institutional interests, the Guggenheim cannot help but project its "Americanness" on the global stage.

"A model of frankness and American pragmatism"

Addressing the question of the Guggenheim's current place and role in U.S. cultural diplomacy, the Guggenheim's Director of Curatorial Affairs, Joan Young, made the point rather explicitly:

> I think, for the Guggenheim, we are less interested in U.S. cultural diplomacy in relation to our engagement with audiences around the world. And our core collections predominantly feature the European artists [. . .] and throughout the history of our collection practices we focused more on international art rather than American [. . .] our efforts in international programming, exhibitions and opening museums in different countries are not necessarily a contribution to the cultural diplomacy of the USA, but more a contribution to the diplomacy of the Arts. (Young 2012)

The Guggenheim stresses the international nature of the museum's collections and audiences, which places it beyond national borders and the government's diplomatic agenda. Global corporatisation strategies and practices brought Guggenheim to the international level and enabled the museum to establish cross-cultural collaborations and exchanges with local communities across continents. These international engagements help the museum fulfil its institutional mission to "preserve, and interpret modern and contemporary art, and explore ideas across cultures through dynamic curatorial and educational initiatives and collaborations" (Guggenheim 2018). However, these international programs are not intended to make a meaningful contribution to the diplomatic agenda of the U.S. In many cases, these international programs have been formed by economic concerns.

Revealing key drivers behind the development of the global corporatisation model, Krens repeatedly emphasised that a global Guggenheim was the result of exogenous factors in a larger international context. "Globalization is not an environment that we are shaping," Krens stressed: "It is being shaped around us. To try to resist these forces, or to somehow pretend they don't exist, I think, is suicidal from an institutional standpoint" (Krens

1999). In numerous interviews, Krens has shared that "he did not create the conditions he has been responding to" (Brenson 2002, 6). Commenting on these conditions, the Honorable Chairman of the Guggenheim's Board of Trustees, Lawson-Johnston (2014), further revealed: "museums face a difficult future [. . .] Expenses escalate while financial support from the government dwindles [. . .] the recent history of the Guggenheim is at heart an exemplary response to external economic pressures" (152).

These economic pressures shape the Guggenheim's far-reaching, international programming, driven by the institutional interests of involved stakeholders. For example, discussing the UBS MAP Global Art Initiative, the Guggenheim sponsorship director explained that the project aimed to reach out to artists and communities "in regions where Guggenheim did not have that expertise and history." However, more importantly, "these were also regions where they (UBS) had limited market penetration" (Lund and Greyser 2015, 11). "As art is becoming more and more of an asset class, UBS is looking to increase our profile in these kinds of special fields of interest," the UBS CEO Jürg Zeltner said. "More and more we are refocusing our strategy to reach emerging markets, and this project seemed like a perfect fit" (Vogel 2012).

Collaboration with the Guggenheim on this project allowed UBS to do more than expand its presence and visibility in new geographic areas. It helped them to understand the local context with regard to the size and scope of their economic opportunities in new markets, as well as to develop more relevant offerings to target local customers. "You can't just do it from a banking perspective," the UBS sponsorship director explained:

> You can't really say that you are local, and you understand the culture. In places like Singapore or Hong Kong that are incredibly diverse both culturally and in terms of ethnicity, one cannot relate to the local community without taking a fuller view of history and culture and art and people making art.
>
> (Lund and Greyser 2015, 18)

The economic agenda of transnational corporate patrons and the museum's growing ambition to represent artists from around the world pushed the Guggenheim to grow further in its reach and visibility across countries. Through global corporatisation, the museum found a way not only to survive but also to thrive in the conditions of neo-liberal globalisation. With a high self-earned revenue and considerable investments from its corporate patrons, the Guggenheim stands out from other museums on the international stage as a viable player in the global economy, independent of the national government.

According to the IRS 990 tax reports from 2001–2012, the average contribution to the annual Guggenheim's budget from government grants amounted to less than 3 per cent. In comparison, the majority of museums around the word are still dependent on their national government's support to varying degrees. For example, approximately 30 per cent of the British Museum's annual budget is provided by grant-in-aid from the U.K. Department for Culture, Media and Sport (British Museum 2014). Direct subsidies from the French government make up half of the Louvre's annual budget (Louvre 2014), and 80 per cent of the annual income is contributed to the State Hermitage Museum from the Russian Federation's federal budget (State Hermitage Museum 2014).

Arguably, the Guggenheim is not only a phenomenon shaped by neoliberal globalisation. Its autonomous position from government support can also be explained by a unique national economic context. In the U.S., museum agency notably emerged due to private initiatives or powerful corporate magnates. For example, Andrew Mellon launched the National Gallery in Washington DC; JP Morgan's successors filled New York's Metropolitan Museum with one of the largest collections in the world. Samuel Kress acquired and distributed art among major national collections and dozens of provincial museums (Arndt 2005, 443). Furthermore, from the very beginning ideas around museums were closely linked to liberal economic values:

> American museums, unlike most European ones, also have their roots in a strain of nineteenth-century political philosophy that specifically sought to marry commerce with spectacle to achieve a form of social engineering (improving the middle class). They have always existed in a capitalist environment of winners and losers.
>
> (Kimmelman 1999, 54)

In the late twentieth century, corporate strategies within American museums have become even stronger. Self-generated revenue has constantly grown as a larger part of annual museum budgets, and engagement with corporations has become even more important (Grincheva 2016). The Guggenheim is a logical product of its national economic and political environment. It represents the inherited ideology of liberalism and the predominantly corporate structure of U.S. cultural institutions.

At the same time, the Guggenheim is the museum in which American commercialism, populism and financial adventurism have achieved their highest level, especially under Krens's leadership. Reflecting on that situation, Kimmelman (1999) explained that "it may be that he [Krens] makes people uncomfortable precisely, because he is pursuing the American cultural system to its inevitable conclusion" (54). The museum represents an ideal symbol of the U.S. market economy – "a natural microcosm of the capitalist system, notorious for its tendency to expand on high returns" (Kozloff 1972, 156).

By going global, the Guggenheim projects the values of a liberal market economy, and in this way contributes to the efforts of the U.S. government in spreading global neo-liberal ideologies and the values of the free market economy. According to the official diplomatic discourse of the U.S., an open world economy can push international relations in a cooperative direction, leading not only to prosperity but also to peace. "Selling liberalism" has always remained a strong component of U.S. diplomacy (Ninkovich 1993, 54). Marketisation and corporatisation "carry with them the legitimacy and taken-for-grantedness of several hundred years of international theorizations about the efficiency of markets" to establish a stable and cooperative world order (Djelic and Sahlin-Andersson 2006). Employing global corporatisation strategies, the Guggenheim symbolises the U.S. market economy on the world stage while indirectly contributing to the national foreign policy agenda.

Nye (2004) argued that global Hollywood is one of the greatest cultural assets of the country – one that helps promote American lifestyle and culture on an international scale. The corporate structure of the Guggenheim and its commitment to serving global audiences, as well as its artistic focus on popular culture, makes it a powerful non-state actor, similar to the most successful Hollywood producers. These private actors enjoy global reach, visibility and high economic profits. In pursuit of their own interests on the world stage, however, they promote American culture and values while projecting soft power without government involvement or patronage. The case of the Guggenheim demonstrates that global corporatisation practices work well to build robust platforms for developing international programming with wide, geographically rich and strong economic returns.

By operating across borders, the Guggenheim does not necessarily aim to build bridges of cross-cultural trust and respect in order to help the U.S. government implement its foreign policy objectives in areas of geopolitical concern. The museum has strong global ambitions to project its own institutional image and power that stretch far beyond the national context. At the same time, the Guggenheim succeeded in spreading global corporatisation practices among museums, projecting neo-liberal ideologies of the U.S. market economy. These new practices have had a profound impact on the development of global trends in museum management. Following the Guggenheim's example, many museums around the world have experimented with new museum designs, expanded their offerings and services to wider audiences and developed partnerships with transnational corporations

(Dolan 1999; Brenson 2002). Guggenheim has become "the leading model of globalization for museums" (Fraser 2006, 149).

While the Guggenheim's international developments have no direct implications for cultural diplomacy, the Krensian economics formula of museum success seems to find its diplomatic manifestation in a different country's context. The following part of the chapter takes readers to contemporary China to explore how global corporatisation, as a museum management trend, facilitates private actors to exercise cultural diplomacy.

Krensian economics redefined: projecting cultural China to the world

In the twenty-first century, China has seen rapid economic, political and even militaristic development. However, in the global community, this rise has been predominantly perceived as a threat, which has motivated China to address these negative perceptions. To rebrand its image on the world stage, the Chinese government has invested considerable resources in its soft power infrastructure (Grincheva and Li 2016). During Xi Jinping's presidency alone, China doubled its budget for projecting its soft power from $4.75 billion in 2011 to $9.5 billion in 2018 (Clover et al. 2018).

The government aims to craft a more favourable image of China as an advanced, civilised, democratic, innovative, open, peaceful and responsible country. More importantly, China intends to catch up in the perceived global cultural competition for international visibility and attraction (Hartig 2016). Numerous newly launched, state-funded programs have offered opportunities for "cultural exchanges with the rest of the world in a joint promotion of cultural prosperity" (Hartig 2016). For example, since 2004 Confucius Institutes have rapidly spread across 146 countries to promote Chinese language, history and culture (Gil 2018).

In the 12th Five-Year Development Plan, issued in 2010, museums gained special recognition through the "Cultural China" image-building scheme (Kong 2015). The scheme delegated a leading role to Chinese museums to exercise cultural diplomacy "in order to demonstrate the glorious and splendid achievement of Chinese civilisation" (Kong 2015, 50). It also offered a wide range of government incentives to facilitate rapid development of the museum industry in the country (Gaskin 2014).

Priority access to state-owned land, tax exemptions and special government awards in recognition of "individuals who have made outstanding contributions to the development of private museums" (State Administration of Cultural Heritage 2010) caused a state-sanctioned boom in the museum industry. From only 45 museums in the 1950s, many of which were destroyed during the Cultural Revolution, China established over

1,000 museums in the 2000s (Hsu 2014). The museum world has grown even larger, with almost 5,000 museums in existence now, significantly exceeding the original government expectations set in 2010 (Statista 2017). More and more private museums are mushrooming in China, facilitated by favourable government real estate deals. For example, in Shanghai the government policies encouraged the development of privately funded museums, such as Rockbund Art Museum, Yuz Museum, Long Museum and Zendai Museum, to name just a few.

At the cost of hundreds of millions of dollars, these museums, funded by the new generation of Chinese billionaires and emerging philanthropists, emulate the Krensian economics formula of museum success. The majority are designed by famous architects, ensuring high visibility in the urban context and inviting larger visitation by locals and tourists. Moreover, these newly developed museums go far beyond the Krensian commercialisation agenda, which rather modestly suggested that "two shopping opportunities and two eating opportunities" could help a museum boost its visitation. The newly emerged museums in China usually form part of larger commercial complexes that combine a large variety of restaurants, shopping malls and even hotels. A good example is the Himalayas Art Center in Shanghai, developed by Zendai Group and designed by renowned Japanese architect Arata Isozaki. The Center houses the Zendai Museum, the Himalayas Theatre and a huge shopping mall with a number of restaurants and coffee shops as well as the Jumeriah Hotel.

While the Guggenheim reinforced its corporate development in response to decreasing government support, in China corporate trends in museum development have been strongly encouraged by the government. New regulations stipulated that museums could legally carry out business activities without violating their non-profit attributes and without departing from their mission. These policies aim to adapt museums to the needs of the cultural and leisure economy and integrate them into the cultural tourism industry (State Administration of Cultural Heritage 2010). Museums are encouraged "to raise funds through multiple channels to promote their own development" (The State Council 2015). Furthermore, the Ministry of Education set new roles for contemporary museums in China to become "cultural carriers" of creative industries and key landmarks in "tourist routes across the country" (Yan 2017).

The Chinese government strives to offer "new opportunities to accelerate the development of the museum's cultural and creative industries in China" (Feng 2015). However, it remains questionable whether newly born museums achieve national government goals to "build a comprehensive resource sharing platform that radiates the whole country and faces the world" in order to "mark the image of Chinese civilization" (State Administration of

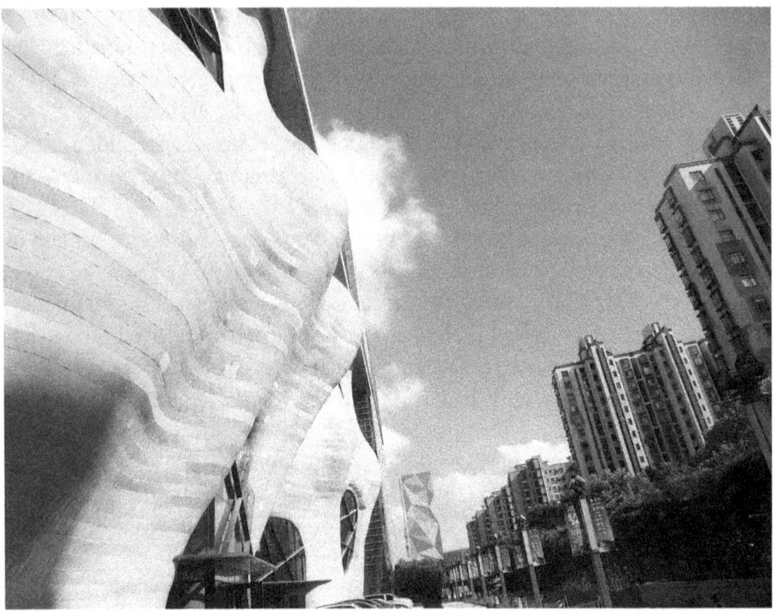

Figure 2.2 Shanghai Himalayas Museum, also known as Zendai Museum (China)

Source: Photograph by Natalia Grincheva, June 2018.

Cultural Heritage 2010). In the same way as the Guggenheim, these new museums are questioned in terms of their artistic excellence and curatorial quality. For instance, Claire Hsu (2014), a founder of the Asia Art Archive in Hong Kong, argues:

> China's current trajectory is too focused on the buildings with little regard for content, too market orientated, and stifled by political constraints. The majority of the art museums being built, while donning the latest architectural coats, are severely lacking in content, programming or qualified professionals, which often come as an after-thought. . . . And most museums double up as rental spaces, which, in effect, means that anyone who can afford to rent the space can have a "museum" show.

The majority of new Chinese museums, indeed, lack sufficient expertise to lead world-class exhibitions that can boast curatorial creativity and excellence of artistic scholarship. In contrast to the Guggenheim, these museums fail to generate high attendance and sustain themselves in the economic sector of culture. They close down as quickly as they pop up in big metropolitan centres and small provincial towns across the country. This situation suggests that Chinese government efforts to maximise cultural influence by reinforcing museum development and corporatisation work quite poorly.

K11 Art Mall, as a culmination of the museum corporatisation trend in China, however, complicates this picture. K11 brings large audiences to its franchise branches, which are rapidly growing in different cities across the country. In the last few years, satellites were established in Shanghai (2013), Hankou (2017), Shenyang and Guangzhou (2018). New branches are planned in Beijing and Tianjin in 2019 (K11 2018). K11 brands itself as an "art playground, where culture, entertainment, shopping and living revolve around art" (K11 2018). Integrating contemporary art into luxury retail spaces, K11 taps into young consumers' expectations in China of enjoying more sophisticated and stimulating cultural experiences, not just shopping opportunities.

The idea of a thematic shopping mall is not new, with Caesars Palace Shopping Center or Tokyo Garden Walk Mall providing evidence of this trend (Ulan 2016). However, integrating an art museum into a shopping mall brings the Guggenheim's global corporatisation model to its absolute conclusion. Art in K11 shopping malls is not strictly confined to dedicated museum or gallery spaces. Instead, it is distributed across all floors of a mall, integrated into interior and exterior design and placed for sale along with other consumer goods. K11 brings together multiple art events and interactives, top floor gardens, multicultural community hubs and large-scale urban design projects. These offerings aim to expand trivial shopping into educational and cultural experiences, bridging the worlds of contemporary arts and commerce.

The central location of K11 malls in each city works in combination with signature architecture buildings that "revitalise and awaken a surrounding urban community" (Ying 2014). At K11, mega-popular transnational luxury brands, such as Dolce & Gabbana and Burberry, coexist with expensive fashionable restaurants as well as contemporary art sculptures, installations and experimental exhibitions. Not only does K11 employ the Krensian economics model to its full extent, it also expands it further, reinforcing the "art-commodity dialectic" of the neo-liberal age. In an interview Adrian Cheng, the founder of K11, explained:

> Well-recognised museums around the world are also involved in retail. Just look at [the] American Museum of Modern Art in New York, the Louvre in France or even the British Museum in London. All of them need to run museum shops, coffee bars and restaurants to generate income. If you can't recognise that K11 is more than just a shopping

> mall, I can't stop you. However, contemporary art is the DNA of the K11 Art Mall concept and it makes its unique.
>
> (Ulan 2016)

In a different interview Cheng also elaborated: "We don't want to just focus on art; we want to cross different segments in the cultural world. We want to cross art with fashion, architecture, furniture, celebrities" (Forbes 2018).

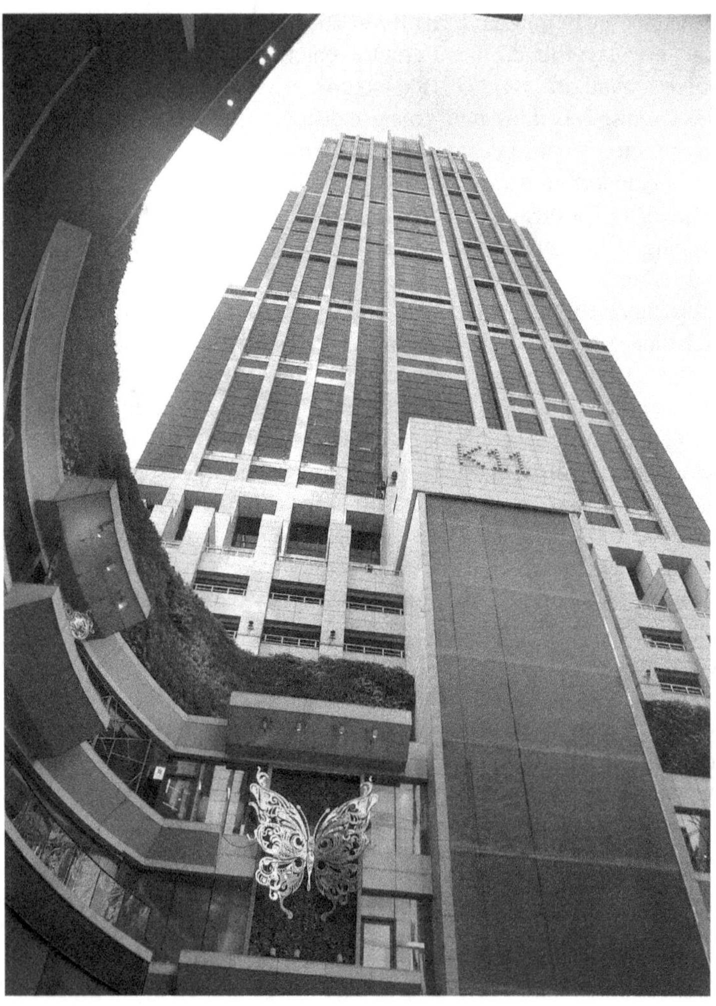

Figure 2.3 K11 Art Mall, branch in Shanghai (China)

Source: Photograph by Natalia Grincheva, June 2018.

Doesn't this combination of contemporary arts, popular culture and global brands of transnational corporations remind us the Guggenheim's blockbusters developed in collaboration with BMW or Giorgio Armani? Challenged with the question of whether K11 could be considered a museum, Cheng confidently argued,

> I think our campaigns and programmes are very similar to those of traditional museums, but there's greater flexibility in terms of the collaborations we can forge and the variety of themes – from Monet, to pop culture, to design, to fashion.
>
> (Cheng 2018)

A retail-based museum, in contrast to a traditional one, does not need to justify its artistic and curatorial choices. It can go for both money and art simultaneously without compromising its status quo as an institution.

Questioning the saneness of the K11 Art Mall idea, Seth Denizen (2015), Professor of Urban Architecture at the University of Hong Kong, pointed out:

> In this vision, the art mall is just the art museum exploded, so that its gift shop and gallery are dispersed homogeneously throughout a single

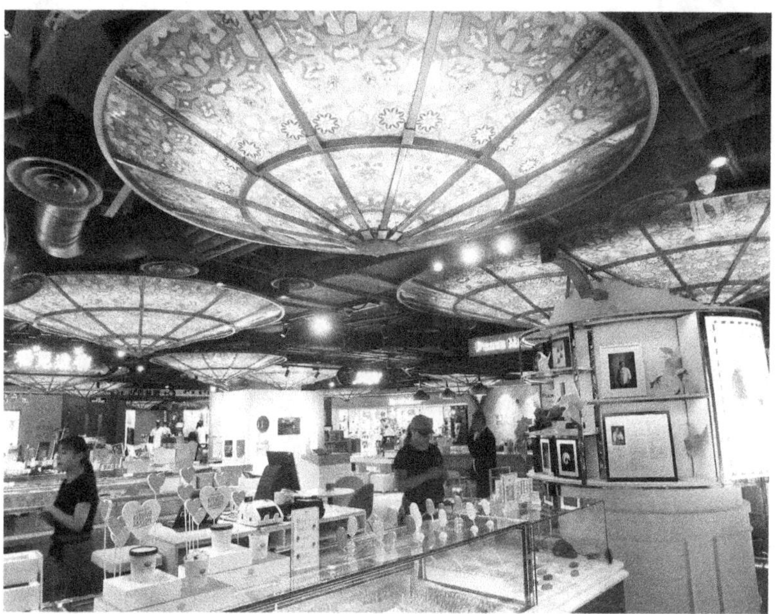

Figure 2.4 K11 Art Mall, interior design, branch in Shanghai (China)

Source: Photograph by Natalia Grincheva, June 2018.

> structure without regard for any cultural conflicts that might result. This non-management of cultural conflict is precisely the utopian architectural proposal of the American mall: everything in one place. Hash pipes and baby carriages. In the wild utopian dreams of the art mall, Hello Kitty tells Claude Monet his paintings are blurry outside their adjacent storefronts. If this sounds like a nightmare to you, that's a common reaction to utopian proposals.

Despite the criticism, K11 Art Malls across China continue to generate high profits, maintaining a growth rate of annual sales at 20 per cent. K11 malls attract a large number of customers, exceeding 1 million per month in the biggest branches located in Hong Kong and Shanghai (Jiafeng 2017). K11 has found its niche and dedicated audiences in not only Hong Kong but also mainland China, because Cheng was able to recognise and satisfy a strong demand among national audiences to consume art and cultural content. This demand was especially strong in conditions in which "art was limited to galleries and auctions, which were inaccessible to the masses, so I thought: 'Why can't we bring art, culture, stories, and curated experiences to a space they feel comfortable in – retail?'" (Cheng 2018).

In recent years, the Chinese government has been unsuccessful in its attempts to change public perceptions of art among national audiences as a "compulsory education" (Yuan 2016). Since 2010, the government has explicitly articulated a need in the cultural sector to increase social participation and promote the cultural value of museums to involve communities in new educational experiences (State Administration of Cultural Heritage 2010). Despite a rapid growth of the museum sector in China, these government aspirations keep challenging the new generation of museums to attract audiences.

For example, in Shanghai, a newly launched, state-run museum – the Power Station of Art – welcomed only 250,000 visitors in 2013. The privately funded Long Museum has attracted no more than 50,000 people since its opening (Caird 2014). In comparison to these visitation records of "pillars in the city's art landscape" (Forbes 2018), the first international exhibition of K11 in Shanghai drew 400,000 people in 100 days. Marking the 50th anniversary of Franco–Sino diplomatic relations, the Monet blockbuster "Master of Impressionism" set a record for visitor attendance at a public exhibition in Shanghai (Zhang 2015).

For this event, K11 built a Japanese bridge at the front of the Mall as well as creating a mini garden with a pool filled with lilies near the gallery space inside the building, thus constructing visual and spatial parallels with Monet's famous painting (Ni 2015). Considering the high cost of the exhibition tickets, the huge popularity of the Monet show demonstrated a strong public demand and thirst for art in China (Ying 2014). "There was the time when we were told by the government what exhibitions we should see," a Chinese artist explained, "Then there was the time when critics and scholars told us what is good and what we should see. Now audiences get to decide what they think is worthwhile by buying tickets to exhibitions" (Zhang 2015).

Since the opening of K11 Art Mall in 2009, the concept of a retail-based museum has been emulated numerous times in China, but in all cases unsuccessfully. In many Chinese museums, the focus on "hardware (architecture, space utilisation, customer services) rather than software (art exhibitions)," as Cheng explained, has kept attendance growth low (Chen and Yong 2016). He further added: "They don't see our hard work behind the scenes on art curation and exhibition management, our core philosophy and a genuine dedication to contemporary arts is not easily transferable as a pure business model" (Chen and Yong 2016). According to its founder, K11's function is not just to bring arts to shopping malls. K11 also intends to turn shopping malls into art museums, to cultivate public taste for art, to support and expose local artists and to build a sustainable local art ecology (Cai 2016).

The key difference between the museum and other spaces, according to Cheng, is its educational function and brand recognition (Jiafeng 2017). This is something that one cannot achieve by focusing only on the business component and maximising economic potential. Recognising that Chinese audiences still need to be educated to appreciate arts and especially contemporary arts, K11's main mission is to bring art to the masses, to make it available, accessible, understandable and desirable for the general public (Ulan 2016). "What we're trying to do is art for the masses," Cheng said. "From 2010, we've been incubating contemporary Chinese artists, curators, and grooming an audience" (Forbes 2018).

The key strategy for the majority of new museums in China has been defined by the formula "put up the museum, put in the collection and then begin to develop what one might call the audience" (Caird 2014). By contrast, Cheng envisions K11's role and its legacy in China "in terms of a broad cultural impact" (Forbes 2018). In fact, he has more ambitious plans for K11 than just generating profitable revenues and engaging young generations of Chinese in new cultural experiences. He aims at no less than projecting the soft power of China to the outside world. He sees K11 as a global player that can establish strong bridges of international exchange, nurturing Chinese art and pushing it to the global stage:

> I hope that K11 can become a soft power symbol of contemporary Chinese art and culture. This is the brand created by Chinese, and I hope it will help Chinese people to communicate their identity and dignity to the global community.
>
> (Chen and Yong 2016)

Such an ambition on the part of a private actor suggests that K11 can be more than just a retail-based museum bringing contemporary arts to the masses in China. The economic power of K11 is strong enough to do more than bring its activities and programming to the international level. It can facilitate productive cross-cultural artistic collaborations between China and the rest of the world by opening up new avenues for cultural diplomacy.

K11 on the global stage: representing Chinese arts to the world

In 2010, Cheng created the K11 Art Foundation (KAF) – a non-profit contemporary arts organisation fully funded by the revenue generated through K11 shopping malls. The foundation's main mission is to promote "the development of the contemporary art scene of Greater China by nurturing artistic talents and taking them to the international stage" (K11 Art Foundation 2016). The KAF runs an artist-in-residence program, which is held at the K11 art village in Wuhan. It organises international exhibitions, workshops and activities in different branches throughout China and is rapidly expanding its international connections.

In the last few years, the Foundation has developed partnerships with numerous well-established museums and cultural intuitions from Western countries. Some of them include Fundaci6 Gala–Salvador Dali in Spain; Serpentine Galleries and the Institute of Contemporary Arts in London; Centre Pompidou, Palais de Tokyo and Musee Marmottan Monet in Paris; and the Metropolitan Museum of Art, the Armory Show, New Museum and the Museum of Modern Art in New York (K11 Art Foundation 2016). Embarking on these international collaborations, the KAF provides a dedicated platform for international exchanges to pursue its mission of strengthening and promoting the Chinese contemporary arts scene globally (K11 Art Foundation 2016).

K11, as a privately owned company, invests its own resources, expertise and efforts in pursuing its goals, which have larger national scope and significance and go far beyond strictly institutional interests. Cheng explained this in the following way:

> Back in 2010 when I founded K11 Art Foundation, there wasn't a platform that supports emerging Chinese artists and curators, so their work couldn't be seen, and they had little support to go national and international. [. . .] But I believe every country needs its art and cultural identity that speaks to its people. [. . .] K11 Art Foundation is a vehicle that propagates Chinese contemporary art, through international

> collaborations, while K11 Art Malls become the stage for everyone to experience the work by these artists and curators.
>
> (Cheng 2018)

In contrast to a traditional museum, K11 has no ambitions to build its own art collection. Instead, it focuses on developing stronger relationships with local and international artists, curators, institutions and audiences. The goal of K11 to provide a robust platform for the global promotion of Chinese arts aligns well with the "going out" government policy. This policy urges museums to "establish a cooperation mechanism with high-level museums abroad" to "enhance the international status, influence and competitiveness of national museums" (State Administration of Cultural Heritage 2010). The implementation mechanism of the "going out" policy outlines the following key objectives: establishing collaboration with world-class experts and scholars, delivering international cultural exchange programs and exhibitions and increasing international cooperation in talent training (State Administration of Cultural Heritage 2010).

Aiming to "promote the outstanding achievements of Chinese culture" (State Administration of Cultural Heritage 2010), however, the "going out" agenda of the Chinese government sets up multiple challenges in the museum sector. It requires significant economic and human resources and expertise, which might not be available to many new, state-owned or private museums across the country. Pioneering a retail-based museum that generates millions of dollars in revenue, Cheng found a solution to the problem. Since the inception of the KAF, he has poured considerable resources into building up its presence in the international art world. He has done so by sponsoring Chinese artists' residencies and exhibitions abroad, supporting a Chinese presence at the most prestigious international arts events, including Venice Biennale and Art Basel, and establishing collaborations with leading museums around the world, such as the Serpentine Galleries, Centre Pompidou and MoMA PS1.

Over the last several years, many of the contemporary art world's best-known curators, such as Hans Ulrich Obrist, Lauren Cornell and Klaus Biesenbach, have collaborated with K11, putting together shows in partnership with leading art institutions around the world. Cheng shared the history of this journey:

> Back in 2013 when I first discussed with Jean de Loisy about working together, K11 and KAF were almost unheard of in the Western world. In five years' time we established ourselves as one of very few celebrated institutions from Asia, the collaborations with American and European museums made us more visible. We act as the bridge between different

> cultures. We tour museum directors and curators in China, bringing them to studio visits and help them better understand the contemporary Chinese art scene. Many of our projects started off with studio visits and ended up in exhibitions, residencies and research projects. I see the relationships as mutual. We bring about cultural exchange and dialogues.
>
> (Cheng 2018)

For example, in 2015 the KAF collaborated with French contemporary art centre Palais de Tokyo to produce the exhibition "Inside China: L'Intérieur du Géant," co-curated by Jo-ey Tang and Wang Chunchen of the Central Academy of Fine Arts Museum in Beijing. It showcased contemporary arts from both countries by featuring works of Renaud Jerez, Nadar and Aude Pariset from France, as well as five Chinese artists – Wu Hao, Yu Ji, Zhao Yao, Cheng Ran, Li Gang and Edwin Lo (Zhang 2015). The exhibition displayed works of Chinese artists who reflected on what was happening "inside China" as well as their French counterparts, whose works expressed "l'intérieur du géant" ("the interior of the Giant"). A reference to the nineteenth-century French photographer and his famous artwork Intérieur du Géant (1863), the French title of the collaborative exhibition served as an allegory for China, the world's largest economy and growing military power (Art Asia Pacific 2015).

This exhibition, as a part of a three-year strategic collaboration between the KAF and the Palais de Tokyo, was dedicated to "the discovery of emerging art scenes in China and France, with a series of presentations in both countries" (Palais de Tokyo 2015). This project explicitly demonstrated the strong capacity of K11 to foster cultural dialogue and boost cross-cultural exchanges between China and other countries. For this project, K11 fully funded Jo-ey Tang, the Hong Kong-born American–French artist and curator, to live in China for a year to explore the contemporary Chinese art scene. Furthermore, "with the support of the K11 Art Foundation and its appointed curator Wang Chunchen," the collaboration was instrumental in organising numerous exhibitions in China and France to promote emerging trends of contemporary Chinese arts (Palais de Tokyo 2015).

Indeed, without generous financial contributions and support from K11, this project would not have been possible. In a private conversation, a curator from another private museum in Beijing shared that she had refused to take the curatorial position at Palais de Tokyo, sponsored by K11, when she was offered this opportunity. As she explained, the controversy around deep pockets that can now shape curatorial decisions in China, and even globally, prevented her from getting involved with the project. "Privately sponsored curators strongly depend on their benefactors. In this case, Mr Cheng had all the power to select Chinese artists to be represented through the international exhibition in France." Leaving aside purely curatorial decisions, it is interesting to observe, in this case, that international collaborations with world leading art institutions are shaped by K11's economic power.

K11 malls, which bring profitable income, provide a robust economic platform for Cheng to establish partnerships with world-recognised museums and cultural institutions. Gregor Muir, previously Executive Director of the Institute of Contemporary Arts (ICA) in London, and currently Director of International Collections at Tate, has pointed out that "with its multi-faceted approach to philanthropy, the KAF continues to build bridges with international museums and organisations in imaginative new ways" (K11 Art Foundation 2015). Having collaborated with K11 on "Enter the Dragon," the first solo U.K. institutional exhibition of Chinese artist Zhang Ding, Muir especially emphasised the scale of the exhibit, which occupied the entire ICA Theatre space in London. He also stressed the "impressive scope" of the international "dynamic new commissions" that K11 could afford (K11 Art Foundation 2015). These projects, at the cost of thousands of dollars, support international exhibitions and cross-cultural residencies of foreign curators to visit China and for Chinese colleagues to travel abroad.

However, K11 invests its own resources to do more than advance its institutional position on the world stage. More importantly, K11 pursues public interests that stand in line with Chinese foreign policy agenda. Cheng stressed:

> We do have a societal mission – to show the world the real China through cultural exchange. People only focus on the rapid economic development of China in recent years, but seldom explore the country from a culture perspective. [. . .] I think most important is whether the cultural exchange brings new values to the society and helps create a better world.
>
> (Cheng 2018)

Indeed, K11 international activities strongly adhere to the "going out" strategy of the Chinese government of promoting national arts and culture through international collaborations and mutually beneficial exchanges (State Administration of Cultural Heritage 2010). Reflecting on the KAF international work in the past several years, K11's artistic director, Venus Lau, stressed that strong institutional connections with foreign counterparts are instrumental to "create invaluable bridges between the Chinese art world and that of the West" (Lau 2018). These bridges not only open China to the larger international community, but also they allow for the development of creative exchanges among countries, peoples and communities. Lau defines this collaborative international work as a cultural translation that is beyond the mere act of verbal interpretations, and is a comprehensive and deep cultural experience of cross-cultural learning (Lau 2018).

K11's international collaborations, two-way residencies and partnerships with leading museums are an important step away from exclusive government-led initiatives in cultural diplomacy that primarily focus on national promotion. Chinese government efforts in diplomacy are frequently criticised in the West as being "ambitious and aggressive" attempts "to assuage concerns of a 'China threat' in the context of the country's increasingly powerful economy and military status on the world" (Hartig 2016, 670). In contrast, K11 partner institutions from the West stress the cultural value of the KAF's international work. For example, Director of MoMA PS1 Klaus Biesenbach explained: "K11 has grown to be our closest collaborator because they do what we do: They have residencies, they do research, they are artist-centric, and they are very generous in giving information out" (Forbes 2018).

Such a favourable appraisal of K11's international engagements by a world-recognised institution marks the emergence of non-state actors in authoritarian China. These private players can now exercise cultural diplomacy more effectively than the national government. As Cheng pointed out: "We are very excited to be building this platform, which we hope will nurture more creative talents from Greater China to be seen, heard and appreciated" (Zhang 2015). Confronted with a direct question of whether K11's international work could be called "cultural diplomacy," Ross Leo, Director of the KAF, responded in the following way:

> We are a private institution, but it would be wrong to say that we are not forming a part of the Chinese or even Asian cultural sector. [. . .] Promoting Chinese contemporary arts and representing the country on the international stage is our "natural" commitment. As a private foundation we aim to pursue our institutional vision and mission, but, in a way, it does tend to adhere to the main aspirations of the Chinese cultural sector. I would not say that this mission could be totally segregated from the national objectives, but the primary focus is on our own work.
>
> (Leo 2018)

While Leo stressed the institutional interests and commitments of the foundation in its pursuit of international engagements, a strict censorship system in China undermines any assertion that these efforts are completely independent. In a private conversation, one of K11's curators said that all exhibitions developed by K11 go through censorship procedures. Artworks and curatorial conceptions need to be approved by the Chinese government before they are permitted to be presented in the public domain. While "there is still a lot of room for critical artistic scholarship," this criticism, as the K11 curator explained, cannot be addressed against the Chinese government.

K11's international cultural exchanges are, indeed, privately funded and are based purely on institutional initiatives. However, the political mechanism of artistic censorship reinforces K11's diplomatic status. Previously, an economic dependency of museums on state funding ensured that museums communicated a positive national image to the outside world. At least, this dependency restricted museums from open criticism of their government. The diplomatic model of K11, however, works differently. In the case of K11, the KAF is not dependent on government funding to go global and implement international programs. Nevertheless, the authoritarian political regime in China enacts strong political control mechanisms that guide the cultural curatorial work of the foundation.

Not only does the censorship ensure that the image of the national government is presented in a favourable way, it also makes the KAF art activities a meaningful part of the national foreign policy agenda. "We do not report to the government on what we are doing here, because we are a private foundation," Leo stressed. However, he added, "we are always open to share our future exhibition plans and ideas." Such a system allows a greater alignment of the foundation's activities and programming with the larger Chinese cultural sector "and makes our own curatorial and research work to be in sync with the national artistic ecosystem" (Leo 2018).

The case of K11 illustrates that a *global corporatisation* museum model could be successfully adopted in the context of China's authoritarian political regime to give birth to a new private or non-state diplomacy. This diplomacy rests on exclusively private economic resources, expertise and ambitions, while directly contributing to the national foreign policy objectives. "Do we consider Hollywood film some kind of cultural diplomacy, propagating the American values to the rest of the world through moving images, or simply a money-making industry that provides entertainment?" Cheng enquired. "How else do you think the rest of the world – especially those who haven't been to the U.S. – get an inkling of the American culture and lifestyle?" (Cheng 2018).

While acknowledging its corporate status as a commercial enterprise, similar to a certain degree to the Hollywood industries, K11 simultaneously commits to making a difference in society to "create a better world" (Cheng 2018). These intentional efforts to promote Chinese artistic excellence and talent on a global level go beyond just maximising economic return. This institutional mission makes K11 an important player in diplomacy.

Moreover, K11's diplomacy works better than government-led diplomatic activities that usually generate controversy and scepticism among global publics. They provide more genuine cultural experiences precisely because they are not initiated or commissioned by the Chinese government, like the Confucius Institutes planted around the world. "Confucius was one of the greatest Chinese philosophers and there is great wisdom in his teaching. That is the old China, it creates a strong foundation," Cheng pointed out. "Whereas through art and culture, K11 is showing the world the contemporary China, present and future. I guess the two are complementary but non-comparable" (Cheng 2018).

The institutional initiatives of K11 on the global stage nicely complement the Chinese government's efforts in cultural diplomacy. For example, the highly successful Monet blockbuster "Master of Impressionism" demonstrated that the Chinese government could even capitalise on these private efforts. As Cheng revealed, even though the Monet exhibition was organised the same year both governments celebrated Franco–Sino diplomatic relations, it was not initially planned as part of the official celebratory program. "It gave us a very good press angle to promote the exhibition, and both the Chinese and French governments were very supportive" (Cheng 2018). This government support is more evidence that K11's international programs stand in sync with the official foreign policy agenda. Privately funded, K11's global activities provide a new avenue for contemporary cultural diplomacy.

Conclusion

This chapter discusses how global corporatisation practices of contemporary museums shape new forms of cultural diplomacy. While the first part on the Guggenheim was instrumental in revealing the economic power of global corporatisation to bring the museum to the global level, the second part on K11 illustrated how this model affects museum diplomacy. Comparing the two cases, it becomes apparent, though, that the global corporatisation model, first successfully trialled by the Guggenheim, has experienced significant expansion and transformation when manifested in the case of K11.

The Guggenheim was established as a museum in which development of the art collection preceded the opening of the actual museum building in New York. The adoption of corporate practices at the Guggenheim was predetermined by its leadership and governance – which, with time, only reinforced its corporate infrastructure and influence. The Guggenheim's commitment to globalism has been instrumental in developing a strong museum brand that can attract powerful international patrons. The global corporatisation model for Guggenheim was a way to strengthen its economic position on the world stage and to pursue its mission to preserve and promote international contemporary arts. It provided the museum with a more sustainable economic platform to initiate and implement projects and exhibitions, reaching audiences across the globe.

Unlike the Guggenheim, K11 was born much later in the conditions of progressed global liberalisation. This case illustrates that the neo-liberal environment strongly affects museum ecosystems, not only in developed economies but also in developing and fast-growing economies such as China. K11 has already emerged as a purely commercial and corporate model that effectively employs art as a means to attract consumers. Furthermore, by contrast with the Guggenheim, K11 is a corporate actor in the first instance. The economic power of K11 relieves it from the need to go around the world in search of wealthy patrons who share similar international expansion interests. Cheng explained:

> We support the non-profit KAF to incubate artists and curators, while KAF provides us with the artistic programs and activities to engage the public. The model is different from a traditional museum or art institution, where they are supported mainly by endowments from trustees.
>
> (Cheng 2018)

Indeed, public museums as non-profit organisations are dependent on their endowments, fuelled by contributions from their Board members. In the case of the Guggenheim, as we have seen earlier, it was important to develop a strong business-oriented governance of the Board. That not only strengthened the endowment through generous commitments of wealthy patrons, but also ensured the corporate development of the museum. Instead, the KAF relies on the corporate revenue of its own shopping malls. This revenue fully supplies necessary resources to keep international art programming of the foundation growing and reaching new geographic horizons. This model allows K11 to secure economic autonomy on the national, and even international, level to implement ambitious cultural projects around the world.

K11's global corporatisation manifests in its shopping malls, which bring together luxury transnational brands and arts under one roof. Profitable revenues generated through K11 shopping malls allow K11 to go global and develop cross-cultural collaboration with major museums around the world. These connections are instrumental for K11 to pursue its ambition to push contemporary Chinese arts to the international level. The global corporatisation model in this case enables the development of a non-state actor of cultural diplomacy that employs private institutional resources, expertise and global connections to project national soft power and promote national artistic talent and culture.

Cheng envisions further development of K11 in the following way:

> The plan is to focus on the expansion of K11 in Greater China. There'll be 29 K11-related projects in nine Chinese cities by 2023. And by K11, I don't mean just Art Malls, but also office buildings, serviced apartments etc. On the software side, the K11 Art Foundation will continue to grow and collaborate with international museums and institutions to propagate Chinese contemporary art.
>
> (Cheng 2018)

As this quote indicates, Cheng primarily seeks the global growth of K11 in its institutional visibility and presence in the international art community. While the business model of K11 is expanding, utilising new commercial opportunities within China, Cheng remains quite confident and consistent in his vision to "propagate Chinese contemporary art" on the international level (Cheng 2018).

Adrian Cheng is not only the founder of K11 but also an active leader of KAF who takes the key curatorial role in establishing international partnerships with museums around the world. He holds a Bachelor of Arts Honours degree from Harvard University and an Honorary Doctorate of Humanities from the Savannah College of Art and Design in the U.S. His personal passion about and commitments to contemporary art in many ways shape the programming of the foundation. Cheng described his role in the development of K11 in the following way:

> If anything, I'm the biggest believer in K11 and I roll the hardest to make sure my team is motivated to be by my side. And at the end of the day, I think it's the passion for art and culture that fuels the growth of K11.
>
> (Cheng 2018)

Unlike Krens, for whom international museum programs were, in some cases, a means to engage with transnational patrons to secure funding, Cheng employs the K11 business model to develop global opportunities for national artists. This mission and commitment make K11 an important actor of non-state cultural diplomacy. This private actor of diplomacy, as the second part of the chapter demonstrated, often outperforms the national government in building meaningful cross-cultural bridges across borders by fully supporting long-term curatorial residencies and artistic exchanges between China and the Western world.

Despite such a strong difference between K11 and Guggenheim, there is something that unites both institutions. It is their economic autonomy from state funding to pursue their institutional interests and commitments on the global stage. Both the Guggenheim and K11 actively employ corporate logic to generate funds that allow them to implement ambitious transnational cultural projects without financial support from their respective national governments. The global corporatisation model brings to life a new type of diplomacy that can rely exclusively on private forces.

In the case of Guggenheim, however, it does not directly translate into programming that could be called cultural diplomacy. The first part of this chapter demonstrated that it is only possible to argue for indirect contributions of the Guggenheim to government efforts in promoting American values of liberalism and global market freedom. The case of K11, however, allows us to extend the argument that the global corporatisation model can be effectively employed to implement diplomacy. As the second part consequently exposed, K11's international cultural messages and vision to push contemporary Chinese arts to the global stage perfectly align with Chinese national strategies and efforts in nation branding and cultural diplomacy.

K11 is one of the first new private diplomatic actors in China, marking a development of the new era in non-state diplomatic practices going beyond the context of Western democracies. Strong political mechanisms in China, however, still deny full autonomy to these actors and restrain their capacities to represent the image of China through more realistic or even critical lenses. Nevertheless, the economic potential of private actors demonstrates the development of the civil society forces, which are gaining more power to initiate cultural exchanges across borders. Museum global corporatisation provides new avenues for cultural diplomacy to reshape relationships among governments, museums and their audiences.

K11 is not only representative of the growing global corporate logic that shapes museum diplomacy in the new century. What remains unexplored in this chapter is the franchise nature of K11 chain. "There is a trend for museums to franchise their brand globally, opening up more spaces in different continents," Cheng pointed out while positively reflecting on this phenomenon.

> At the end of the day, the general public will benefit from this, being able to see and learn more in their home town without traveling all the way to New York or Paris or London. Perhaps that is the way to move forward.
>
> (Cheng 2018)

The next chapter will further investigate the Guggenheim franchise developments that influenced diplomatic practices across museums. It will move away from K11 to analyse the State Hermitage Museum in Russia and its International Network of Foundations to further question the adoptability of the Guggenheim's practices in multiple cultural and political contexts.

References

Arndt, Richard. 2005. *First Resort of Kings: American Cultural Diplomacy in the 20th Century*. Washington, DC: Potomac Books.

Art Asia Pacific. 2015. Review: "Inside China – L'Intérieur du Géant (Hong Kong Station)" @ K11 Art Foundation, Hong Kong. https://bit.ly/2zMsMg9 (accessed November 2018).

Brenson, Michael. 2004. *Acts of Engagement: Writings on Art, Criticism, and Institutions, 1993–2002*. Lanham, MD: Rowman & Littlefield.

British Museum. 2014. Annual Report 2013–2014. https://bit.ly/2SvUrZL (accessed March 2015).

Cai, Meng. 2016. Zheng Zhigang: Enhancing the Country's Soft Power and Promoting Chinese Contemporary Art to the World. *Chinese Culture News*, 28 September. https://bit.ly/2rnMvyp (accessed November 2018).

Caird, Jo. 2014. The Future of Museums in China. *Guardian*, 6 February. https://bit.ly/2zNBr26 (accessed November 2018).

Chen, Xuehui and Yuan Yong. 2016. K11: Art and Business Combination: Interview with Adrian Cheng. *Economic Daily*, 8.

Cheng, Adrian. 2018. Interview by Natalia Grincheva.

Clover, Charles and Sherry Fei Ju. 2018. China's Diplomacy Budget Doubles Under Xi Jinping. *Financial Times*, 6 March. https://on.ft.com/2EiTTDB (accessed November 2018).

Conn, Steven. 2010. *Do Museums Still Need Objects?* Philadelphia: University of Pennsylvania Press.

Cuno, James. 2001. A World Changed? Art Museums After September 11. *Bulletin of the American Academy of Arts & Sciences* 55(4): 17–36.

Davis, John. 1994. *The Guggenheim: An American Epic*. New York, NY: SP Books.

Denizen, Seth. 2015. In Defence of the Art Mall. *Asia Art Archive*. https://bit.ly/2RDTKNX (accessed November 2018).

Djelic, Marie-Laure and Kerstin Sahlin-Andersson. 2006. *Transnational Governance. Institutional Dynamics of Regulation*. Cambridge: Cambridge University Press.

Dolan, David. 1999. Cultural Franchising, Imperialism and Globalisation: What's New? *International Journal of Heritage Studies* 5(1): 58–64.

Fabelová, Karolína. 2010. Museums for Sale: The Louvre and Guggenheim in Abu Dhabi New Presence. *The Prague Journal of Central European Affairs* 12(2): 53–58.

Feng, Ding. 2015. The Museum Regulations Officially Implemented the Development of China's Cultural and Creative Industries and Ushered in the Policy "Accelerator." *Xinhuanet*, 20 March. https://bit.ly/2RFtjaR (accessed November 2018).

Forbes, Alexander. 2018. Adrian Cheng Is Building a New Culture for Chinese Millennials – One Art Mall at a Time. *Art Market*, 22 March. https://bit.ly/2G4P5DD (accessed November 2018).

Fraser, Andrea. 2006. Isn't This a Wonderful Place? (A Tour of a Tour of the Guggenheim Bilbao). In *Museum Frictions*, eds. Ivan Karp and Corinne Kratz, 135–160. Durham, NC: Duke University Press.

Gaskin, Sam. 2014. China's Aggressive Museum Growth Brings Architectural Wonders. *CNN*, 30 April. https://cnn.it/2EgpvtF (accessed November 2018).

Gil, Jeffrey. 2018. Why the NSW Government Is Reviewing Its Confucius Classrooms Program. *The Conversation*. https://bit.ly/2AZZQB4 (accessed November 2018).

Gomez, Edward. 2002. If Art Is a Commodity, Shopping Can Be an Art. *New York Times*, 8 December, 43.

Grincheva, Natalia. 2016. Museum Dimension of American "Soft Power": Genealogy of Cultural Diplomacy Institutions. In *"Hearts and Minds": US Cultural Management in Foreign Relations in the 21st Century*, ed. Matthew Chambers. Frankfurt am Main: Peter Lang.

Grincheva, Natalia and Jenny Lu. 2016. BRICS Summit Diplomacy: Constructing National Identities through Russian and Chinese Media Coverage of the Fifth BRICS Summit in Durban, South Africa. *Global Media and Communication Journal* 12(1): 1–23.

Guggenheim, Peggy. 2001. The Art of the Motorcycle. http://bit.ly/1It8maY (accessed March 2015).

Guggenheim, Peggy. 2013. Architecture. http://bit.ly/1akZsu2 (accessed March 2015).

Guggenheim, Peggy. 2018. About Us. www.guggenheim.org/about-us (accessed November 2018).

Haacke, Hans. 2012. The Guggenheim Museum: A Business Plan. *Springerin*, 7 September.

Hartig, Falk. 2016. How China Understands Public Diplomacy: The Importance of National Image for National Interests. *International Studies Review* 18: 655–680.

Havis, Richard James. 2015. Interview: Alexandra Munroe, Guggenheim's Asia Art Chief. http://bit.ly/2dUo0Tj (accessed October 2016).

Hsu, Claire. 2014. What Does China's Art Boom Tell Us About Its Society? *World Economic Forum*. https://bit.ly/2PlaBU1 (accessed November 2018).

Hughes, Thomas. 2010. Social Media Spotlight: The Guggenheim and YouTube Play. Technology in the Arts. http://bit.ly/1FPMYdH (accessed March 2015).

Jiafeng, Bai. 2017. Interview with Fritz Huang. *Art China*, 1. https://bit.ly/2QmQxGg (accessed November 2018).

K11. 2018. About K11. https://news.k11.com (accessed November 2018).

K11 Art Foundation. 2015. *Art Diary*. Hong Kong: K11.

K11 Art Foundation. 2016. *Art Diary*. Hong Kong: K11.

Kimmelman, Michael. 1999. The Globe-Straddler of the Art World: the Guggenheim's Thomas Krens. *Museum International* 51(1): 51–55.

Kimmelman, Michael. 2002. An Era Ends for the Guggenheim. *The New York Times*, 6 December.

Kong, Da. 2015. *Imaging China: China's Cultural Diplomacy Through Loan Exhibitions to British Museums*. University of Leicester.

Kozloff, Max. 1972. The Trouble of Art as Idea. *Art Forum* 11(1): 33–37.

Krauss, Rosalind. 1990. The Cultural Logic of the Late Capitalist Museum. *The MIT Press* 54(1): 3–17.

Krens, Thomas. 1999. Lecture at the Art Show. Manhattan's Seventh Regiment Armory, New York, 20 February, Brenson 2002.

Lau, Venus. 2018. Interview by Natalia Grincheva.

Lawson-Johnston, Peter. 2014. *Growing Up Guggenheim: A Personal History of a Family Enterprise*. New York, NY: Open Road Media.

Leo, Ross. 2018. Interview by Natalia Grincheva.

Loughery, John. 2001. The Future of Museums: The Guggenheim, MoMA, and the Tate Modern. *The Hudson Review* 53(4): 631–638.

Louvre. 2014. Annual Report 2014. http://bit.ly/2tPg9Mp (accessed March 2015).

Lund, Ragnar and Stephen A. Greyser. 2015. *Corporate Sponsorship in Culture*. Harvard Business School.

Mathur, Saloni. 2005. Social Thought and Commentary: Museums and Globalization. *Anthropological Quarterly* 78(3): 3697–3708.

McClellan, Andrew. 2008. *The Art Museum from Boullée to Bilbao*. Berkeley, CA: University of California Press.

McLaughlin, Derina. 1997. Is the Development and Touring of the Blockbuster Exhibition in Australian Museum and Science Centers a Long-Term Strategy? *National Museums Australia Conference proceedings*. Melbourne, VIC: Australian Museums and Galleries Association.

Metropolitan Museum. 2011–2015. IRS 990-tax Reports: Metropolitan Museum. http://bit.ly/2wcM5LH (accessed July 2016).

Munroe, Alexandra. 2012. Public Panel Discussion Recorded at the Jim Thompson Art Center in Bangkok on November 28. https://bit.ly/2AX8u3t (accessed March 2015).

Ni, Wu. 2015. China Has Its Monet Moment. *PressReader*, 24 March.

Ninkovich, Frank. 1993. *The Diplomacy of Ideas: U.S. Foreign Policy and Cultural Relations, 1938–1950*. Cambridge, MA: Cambridge University Press.

Nye, Joseph. 2004. *Soft Power: The Means to Success in World Politics*. New York, NY: Public Affairs.

O'Brien, Thomas. 1989. Rich Beyond the Dreams of Avarice: The Guggenheims in Chile. *Business History Review* 63(1): 122–159.

Packer, Jeremy. 2008. *Mobility Without Mayhem: Safety, Cars, and Citizenship*. Dunham, NC: Duke University Press.

Palais de Tokyo. 2015. Inside China L'Intérieur du Géant. https://bit.ly/2UhuAGG (accessed November 2018).

Potvin, John. 2012. Fashion and the Art Museum: When Giorgio Armani Went to the Guggenheim. *Journal of Curatorial Studies* 1(1): 47–63.

Rectanus, Mark. 2002. *Culture Incorporated: Museums, Artists and Corporate Sponsorship*. Minneapolis, MN: University of Minnesota.

Rogers, David, Vrotsos, Karen and Bernd Schmitt. 2003. *There's No Business That's Not Show Business: Marketing in an Experience Culture*. New York, NY: FT Press.

Sorkin, Michael. 2005. Brand Aid or The Lexus and the Guggenheim (Further Tales of the Notorious B.I.G. ness). In *Commodification and Spectacle in Architecture*, ed. William Saunders, 22–33. Minneapolis, MN: University of Minnesota Press.

Sheller, Mimi and John Urry. 2004. *Tourism Mobilities: Places to Play, Places in Play*. London: Routledge.

State Administration of Cultural Heritage (SACH). 2010. Ministry of Long-Term Development Plan for the Career of the Museum (2011–2020). https://bit.ly/2AWojHN (accessed November 2018).

The State Council. 2015. The People's Republic of China. State Council Order. No. 659. Museum Regulations. https://bit.ly/2BVCheM (accessed November 2018).

State Hermitage Museum. 2014. Annual Report 2013–2014. http://bit.ly/2tON0Fh (accessed July 2017).

Statista. 2017. Number of Museums in China from 2007 to 2017. https://bit.ly/2rodf1y (accessed November 2018).

Sylvester, Christine. 2009. *Art/Museums: International Relations Where We Least Expect It*. London: Paradigm Publishers.

Trilupaityte, Skaidra. 2009. Guggenheim's Global Travel and the Appropriation of a National Avant-Garde for Cultural Planning in Vilnius. *International Journal of Cultural Policy* 15(1): 123–138.

Ulan. 2016. K11 Art Mall: An Innovative Template for Art-Themed Shopping Centers. *China Apparel*. https://bit.ly/2BUPvIp (accessed November 2018).

Vail, Karole. 2009. *The Museum of Non-Objective Painting: Hilla Rebay and the Origins of the Solomon R. Guggenheim Museum*. Solomon R. Guggenheim Foundation.

Vivant, Elsa. 2011. Who Brands Whom? The Role of Local Authorities in the Branching of Art Museums. *Town Planning Review* 82(1): 99–115.

Vogel, Carol. 1998. Latest Biker Hangout? Guggenheim Ramp. *The New York Times*, 3 August.

Vogel, Carol. 2012. Guggenheim Project Challenges "Western-Centric View." *Art & Design*, 11 April.

Watkin, David. 1991. Frank Lloyd Wright & The Guggenheim Museum. *AA Files* 21(1): 40–48.

Yan, Huang. 2017. Exploring the Development of Museums from the Current National Cultural Tourism Policy. *Art Education* 16: 149–152.

Ying, Lin. 2014. K11: The Idea Is Reflected in Every Detail. *China Advertising*, 8. https://bit.ly/2E52Yil (accessed November 2018).

Young, Joan. 2012. Interview by Natalia Grincheva.

Yuan, Yi. 2016. The Audience of Our Museum Has Nearly Doubled in the Past Six Years. The Concept of Exhibition Is Still in the "Initial Stage." *Xinhua News Agency*, 20 May. https://bit.ly/2Qfd1Zq (accessed November 2018).

Zhang, Kun. 2015. Shanghai's Thirst for Art. *China Daily*, 12 September.

3 Museum diplomacy as a global franchise

A well-recognised brand has become a necessity for contemporary museums striving to promote their distinctive identities, collections and programming amid the competition of the global cultural marketplace. To boost their brands, museums widely utilise touring international blockbusters, eye-catching architectural designs and special offerings ranging from late-night receptions to concerts. But none of these strategies can compete with museum franchising. Museum franchising is the culmination of global changes in the management of museums (Werner 2005). Opening new branches in different geographical locations allows a museum to establish its presence and visibility among new audiences, to increase its global recognition and to promote its brand far beyond its home location.

Museum franchising has proven to be a more economically effective model of strategic development and management of institutional resources, as well as cultural programming and fundraising activities (Fabelová 2010; Vivant 2011; Wu 2002). Through franchising, museum collections can be loaned and circulated across branches in an easier and more organised manner. "The franchise plan does help to overcome the misallocation of resources which [. . .] is implied by large, underplayed reserves of art" (Heilbrun 2010, 73). Museum franchising also provides opportunities for trading curatorial services to their branches, thus generating income through sharing the museum's cultural expertise (Heilbrun 2010). Furthermore, by relying on the support of local stakeholders, museum branches in different countries significantly strengthen museum global fundraising by attracting new powerful patrons and investment opportunities from across borders (Grincheva 2017).

The Guggenheim Museum's international expansion after 1990 most vividly represents the new model of museum management in the context of neo-liberal globalisation. Its operating branches in Venice (1951) and Bilbao (1997), the now-closed satellites in Berlin (1997–2013) and Las Vegas (2001–2007) and numerous attempts to establish new franchises across continents from Rio to Singapore have transformed the museum. With

Thomas Krens, the Guggenheim grew from a New York-based museum into a global brand, constantly expanding to new cultural markets. "Without global growth," the former Chair of the Board of Trustees pointed out, "[the] Guggenheim in New York would be a substantially poorer institution – financially and artistically – and clearly would serve the public interests less fully" (Lawson-Johnston 2014, 136).

While the Guggenheim franchising activity is constantly declining with the most recent withdrawal of the Helsinki project (2016) and uncertainties around the future branch in Abu Dhabi, franchising is setting global trends in the world of contemporary museums. In past decades, museums such as Tate, Pompidou, Louvre, Getty, Paley Center, Reina Sofia and many others were caught up in franchising experiments, with varying degrees of success. Indeed, cultural franchising continues to grow and be transformative, now affecting museums in developed countries beyond the Western world. The International Network of Museum Foundations, established by the State Hermitage Museum in Russia, provides good evidence of this trend. One of the largest art museums in the world and the most important icon of Russian culture, history and heritage, the Hermitage is among the few museums globally to successfully employ, and even advance, the Guggenheim franchise model.

Since the 1990s, the Hermitage has been developing an International Network of Foundations in different corners of the world. The Network includes the Foundation Hermitage Friends in the Netherlands founded in 1994; the American Friends of the State Hermitage Museum established in 1995; the State Hermitage Museum Foundation of Canada created in 1997; and the U.K. Friends of the Hermitage registered in 2003. More recently, new Hermitage Foundations were established in Italy in 2012, in Israel in 2013 and in Finland in 2016. Furthermore, the network includes museum franchise branches, such as Hermitage Amsterdam (2004) in the Netherlands, Hermitage Kazan (2005) in Tatarstan and two new expansion projects, Hermitage Barcelona and Hermitage Shanghai. New branches in Russia are also developing in Yekaterinburg, Omsk, Vladivostok and Moscow.

"Opening of the new centres is an absolutely unique thing," Director of the Hermitage, Mikhail Piotrovsky, stressed; "unfortunately, few people understand [this]." Reflecting on the global picture of museum franchise strategy, he further added: "Only in a small number of museums we have brilliant results, in general this experiment was conducted without use" (Mamaeva 2017). The Hermitage global network is a thriving and constantly developing chain of foundations and branches. It is a convincing example of the *museum franchising* model that works, grows in time and expands to new geographies. Furthermore, it proves that franchising can be more than just a project of neo-colonisation as criticised in academia, mostly in relation to the Guggenheim (Rauen 2001; Sorkin 2005). This chapter traces the development of museum franchising from the Guggenheim to the Hermitage. It argues that the Guggenheim's global expansion strategy has successfully re-emerged in the context of the State Hermitage Museum. Moreover, it gave birth to a new form of cultural diplomacy in authoritarian Russia.

The first sections of the chapter will document the development of the museum franchise, exposing controversies associated with global McDonaldisation of the Guggenheim. However, the second part will reveal the success of the franchising model re-adapted by the State Hermitage to establish fruitful bridges of cross-cultural engagements. These interactions across borders, facilitated by the Hermitage International Network, build new avenues for cultural diplomacy, bypassing control of the Russian government. Like in the case of K11, the example of the State Hermitage reveals the emergence of new powerful non-state actors of diplomacy within authoritarian political regimes. Comparing the Guggenheim and Hermitage cases, the chapter traces the evolution of museum franchising from a mere global expansion and branding strategy to a powerful international relationship-building tool complementing national efforts in cultural diplomacy.

The global Guggenheim: developing international franchise

While the Guggenheim franchise is usually associated with Krens's bold strategy of global expansion, in fact, the first international museum branch came to the Guggenheim "as a stroke of sheer nepotistic luck" (Decker 2008, 124). The first museum that came under the umbrella of the Solomon R. Guggenheim Museum was the Peggy Guggenheim Museum in Venice. Unlike all other satellite museums, it was inherited from Peggy Guggenheim, niece to Solomon Guggenheim and daughter of Benjamin Guggenheim, who had dedicated herself to collecting modern European art. Exhibited at the 1948 Venice Biennale, her collection of Cubist, Surrealist and European abstract paintings and sculptures gained world recognition. Peggy Guggenheim purchased the Palazzo Venier dei Leoni on Venice's Grand Canal in Venice and permanently installed her collection there.

Two years before her death, she was invited to the museum in New York to exhibit her collection, where she resolved to donate her palace and works of art to the Solomon R. Guggenheim Foundation. However, this donation came under the agreement that "nothing in the Collection could be de-accessioned, and its entirety was to remain on display in the Venice palace" (Guggenheim 1987, 182). That agreement gave birth to the first Guggenheim museum branch in Europe, officially opened under the management of the Foundation in New York in 1980. Bringing more than 175,000 visitors a year to its relatively modest exhibition space, the new

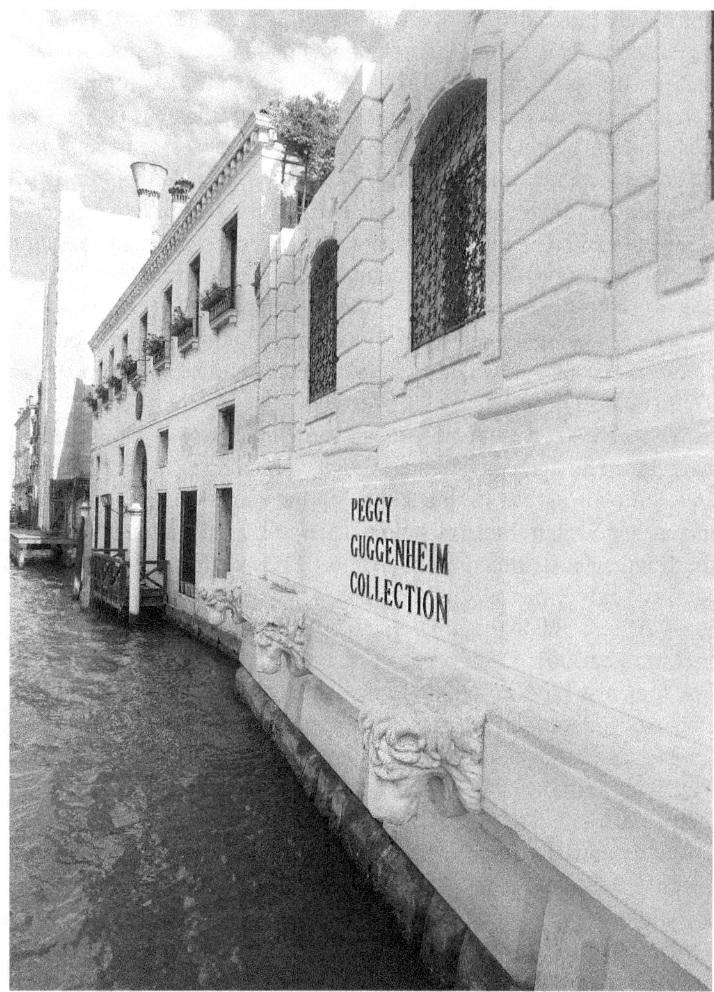

Figure 3.1 Peggy Guggenheim Collection, Venice (Italy)

Source: "Home of the Peggy Guggenheim Collection" by Alistair Young, www.flickr.com/photos/ajy/4890825625 Licence at https://creativecommons.org/licenses/by-sa//2.0/

branch in Venice became the Guggenheim's initial step toward European expansion (Guggenheim 1993, 34). It inspired more ambitious plans to go global, as Krens remarked, the "need to have more and at a larger scale" (Krauss 1990).

By the end of the 1980s, the Guggenheim recognised the strong potential of a fully integrated international institution situated in several places (Guggenheim 1993, 34). But it took almost another decade to open another branch in Europe. Guggenheim Bilbao marked the development of the first franchise museum in the world. Although Bilbao was not Krens's first choice for hosting a franchise, the museum possessed funds specifically designated for urban renewal. Conceived as a partnership between the Solomon R. Guggenheim Foundation and the Basque government, the Guggenheim Bilbao aimed to contribute to an economic regeneration plan for the largest city in the Basque country (Guggenheim 2000a). It intended to transform the "deteriorated port, gravely afflicted by accumulated debts, a 25 percent unemployment rate, industrial pollution and outmoded steel and iron trades" into one of the best cultural destinations in Europe (Bradley 1997, 48).

In October 1991, Krens and Joseba Arregi, then Basque cultural commissioner, signed an agreement, entering into a binding 20-year contract. The Basque officials agreed to finance the entire operation, in which the total costs reached $250 million, including a $20 million donation or "rental fee" to the Guggenheim (Rauen 2001). Although the project was expensive, the feasibility study projected that the museum would generate a high attendance of at least 500,000 annual visitors, bringing around $14 million per year (Martinez 2001, 33).

The franchise model established the Guggenheim's central control of the Bilbao museum's collection acquisitions, management services, educational programs, curatorial research and programming and even human resource management (Bradley 1997, 48). Such a model ensured the Guggenheim Bilbao would be built to the standard of Krens's museum success formula. The first essential element in this success model was based on establishing fruitful and long-term collaboration with powerful authorities abroad that could make considerable investment in the franchise project. The second was creating the "signature" architecture of the new museum to make the site an unforgettable experience. Finally, the new Guggenheim satellite museum had to be opened with a popular exhibition to generate mass audience appeal and interest. Krens emphasised: "If the art can match the architecture, then we will have a defining moment here" (Bradley 1997).

Designed by Frank Owen Gehry, the famous architect of world-renowned tourist attractions, the 336,000-square-foot Guggenheim Bilbao became a desirable world destination long before the museum first opened its doors (Vivant 2011). Situated downtown on the banks of the Nervion River, the museum offered an "open celebration of the supremacy of sight" and "a genetic mutation so spectacular that not even the most reckless of scientists could ever have imagined." The city of Bilbao, "once the 'forge' of Spain, has become a single, great museum" (dal Col and Forster 1998, 98). With no other major tourist attraction in the area, the Guggenheim's iconic architecture was the key to the success of the Guggenheim Bilbao, which still attracts, on average, a million visitors a year and reached 1,322,611 visitors in 2017 (Statista 2018).

Without direct investment costs from the Guggenheim itself, the satellite museum significantly strengthened the institutional budget and expanded the Guggenheim's exhibitory spaces abroad. But, more importantly, it proved that Krens's idea of global expansion could be successfully implemented. He had created "a new historic reality. The Guggenheim-Bilbao proves that the 'global' museum can work," Joseba Zulaika wrote. Zulaika (2001) has researched the Guggenheim Bilbao for many years and had an opportunity to hear Krens talk about the museum: "Money is not important," he said. "The important thing is that now we know that transnational museums are viable" (Zulaika 2001, 112).

The Guggenheim Bilbao not only met the expectations of the Basque government but also significantly exceeded the initial assessments of its economic return. Starting from its first year of operation, the Bilbao museum attendance figures almost tripled the original projected numbers. In 1998, 1.3 million people visited the Guggenheim Bilbao, and in 1999, the attendance reached 1.1 million (Mediguren 2001). These visitors had a positive effect on the city's economy, improving the general level of tourism –

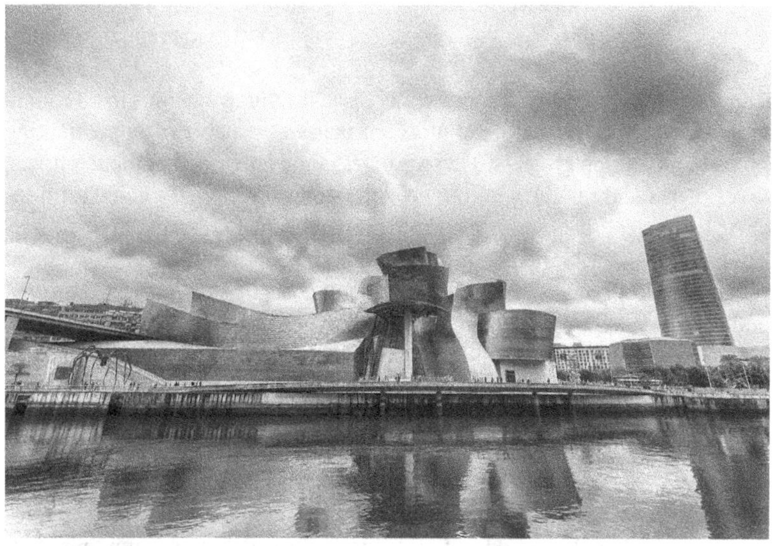

Figure 3.2 Guggenheim Bilbao, Bilbao (Spain)

Source: "Museo Guggenheim Bilbao" by José Jiménez – Astromet, www.flickr.com/photos/astromet/36036404942 Licence at https://creativecommons.org/licenses/by-sa//2.0/

which increased nearly 120 per cent (Ellis 2007). In the first years of its operation, the museum employed more than 4,415 local residents in various capacities (Mediguren 2001). A 1998 economic report revealed that museum visitors "had spent over €50 million on accommodations, €14 million on transportation, €80 million on entertainment, €62 million on shopping, and €30 million at the museum itself on ticket sales, shopping, and at the museum restaurant" (Marwick 1998).

The economics of the Guggenheim Bilbao's impact on urban development suggested the power of the museum's brand to promote the city as a tourist destination (Bradley 1997; Decker 2008; Vivant 2011). The museum in Bilbao, with its almost immediate economic return on investments, gave rise to a so-called Bilbao effect that echoed around the world in many cities. Following the success of the Bilbao franchise, many cities began to evaluate their investment capacities to invite a new branch of the Guggenheim to their location (Trilupaityte 2009, 125). In a Guggenheim press release, published in 2000, Krens noted:

> Since the opening of the Guggenheim in Bilbao in late 1997, the interest in what has come to be known as "the Bilbao effect" has grown exponentially. Between Frank's office and mine, we have received more than 60 requests to participate in urban development and cultural infrastructure projects from institutions, cities, and regional governments all over the world.
>
> (Guggenheim 2000b)

The success of its Bilbao franchise increased the Guggenheim's institutional confidence to brand itself as a museum that was capable of implementing urban regeneration projects. These projects aimed to bring in global tourists, investments and rapid economic growth. Krens developed a standard franchise agreement that was proposed to all who wanted to assess their capacities to build a new branch in their location. The conditions of this agreement obliged future franchise owners to cover all costs of new museum building and to secure approximately $50 million to acquire a new collection. This collection should, however, conform to the Guggenheim standards set in New York. More importantly, the franchise agreement obliged local stakeholders to pay franchise fees to the Guggenheim, ranging between $20 million and $30 million (Lawson-Johnston 2014).

Inspired by the "Bilbao effect," many local authorities were interested in opening Guggenheim branches as a way to revitalise their local economies. Even cities that could not afford to build a global museum "pick[ed] up on the Guggenheim regeneration idea" (Sylvester 2009, 135). The Bilbao example suggested that by using the Guggenheim's brand, cities could enhance their global visibility as appealing tourist destinations. Furthermore, under the umbrella brand of the famous Guggenheim, a completely new museum could promote itself as "an inevitable and legitimate cultural institution" (Vivant 2011, 113).

Despite huge interest in developing the Guggenheim branches across continents, not all ambitious franchise ideas have been implemented. Most cities gave up the idea after conducting feasibility studies and realising the high cost of such a project. For example, the city of Seoul signalled a strong interest in building a satellite museum, but got caught up in the Asian economic crisis of 1997–1998. Prospective Guggenheim franchises also emerged in Singapore and Hong Kong, but were eventually abandoned because of economic constraints (Fabelová 2010, 55). Urban development and regeneration projects enthusiastically commenced in Guadalajara, Mexico and Taichung, Taiwan. Both cities envisioned construction of a Guggenheim branch as an effective means to boost their local economies through tourism development. However, these projects eventually fizzled out as the cities struggled with construction costs and funds deficiency (Decker 2008).

Whether these franchising projects were successful or not, the Guggenheim brand was rapidly gaining value and increasingly being recognised across the world. These franchise initiatives did not require financial investments from the museum side. Moreover, these projects were primarily initiated by local authorities in different cities and closed due to internal problems and economic instability, rather than any fault attributable to the Guggenheim. As a result, the franchise failures around the world hardly hurt the reputation of Guggenheim (Vivant 2011). For example, in relation to the closure of the Rio project, Krens optimistically remarked: "If it doesn't happen, it wouldn't be the first time I didn't get what I wanted [. . .] We've produced an exquisite concept for a museum in South America and we've been compensated for that," referring to the $2 million fee received by the museum for conducting a feasibility study in Rio (Rosenbaum 2003, 46).

In the beginning of the 2000s, the Guggenheim franchise idea remained quite popular and appealed to potential international investors seeking powerful urban regenerations tools. One of the largest of such ongoing projects is Guggenheim Abu Dhabi, a partnership with the Arab Emirate's Tourism Development & Investment Company. Initiated in 2006, Abu Dhabi Guggenheim was conceived as the largest and most expensive franchise project of urban regeneration. Over the past two decades, the Abu Dhabi government has invested considerable resources and efforts to transform the city from a "laid back" metropolis to a centre for arts and innovation – globally, locally and within the wider Middle East (Elsheshtawy 2012). In order to attain world city status, as well as establish regional dominance in attracting foreign talent and global tourists, the Abu Dhabi government focused on culture-based urban development.

The Abu Dhabi Vision 2030, the plan for building a cultural district, draws on key components of Krensian economics. It stresses the city's urban growth through ambitious architectural projects in which spectacular architecture and museum spaces take the central role. For example, Saadiyat Island is "a $27 billion luxury property development on a once-uninhabited sandbar just off the Abu Dhabi coastline" (Wyma 2014). It is designed to house the "international artistic achievements and architectural excellence" of three global museums – the Louvre Abu Dhabi (2017), Zayed National Museum and the Guggenheim Abu Dhabi (Abu Dhabi Tourism & Culture Authority 2017), all commissioned to be built by world-renowned architects.

In July 2006, the Arab Emirate's government and the Guggenheim signed an agreement to establish a world-class museum to feature global art, exhibitions and education programs particularly focusing on Middle Eastern contemporary art. On the day of signing the contract, His Highness Sheikh Mohammed Bin Zayed Al Nahyan, Crown Prince of Abu Dhabi, announced: "Today's signing represents the determination of the Abu Dhabi government to create a world-class cultural destination [. . .] of international standing, one capable of achieving and maintaining relationships with the very highest caliber of global partners." In response, Krens acknowledged the importance of this partnership:

> In Abu Dhabi we have had the good fortune to discover a partner that not only shares our point of view but expands upon it. The plans for Saadiyat Island and the cultural district [. . .] are, quite simply, extraordinary.
> (Guggenheim 2006)

Indeed, this was the first Guggenheim franchise project with such "extraordinary" resources and investment capabilities. For example, as a part of the deal, the new branch committed to develop a collection with a budget of up to $600 million, which exceeded by 200 times the annual acquisitions budget of the Guggenheim in New York (Ourossof 2010). The new satellite was envisioned to be the largest ever built by the Guggenheim, covering 450,000 square feet. The architectural design of the museum building was again commissioned to Frank Owen Gehry, continuing the same brand development strategy with a focus on signature architecture (Guggenheim 2006).

Despite these ambitious plans, in the last 13 years the construction of the new Guggenheim branch in Abu Dhabi has been constantly delayed. More importantly, the future of the new branch has not been clear – as evidenced in a public announcement made by Krens in 2017, which favoured a scaling back of the whole project. "It may not be such a good idea these days to have an American museum, essentially with a Jewish name, in the country that does not recognize Israel," Krens stressed in disapproval of the project (Abrams 2017). As he further explained, the plans for the museum were conceived in more naïve times, when globalisation in the art world was less politicised in contrast to the current political climate. "The world financial crisis and the Arab Spring has changed the equation radically," Krens emphasised.

Despite the pessimism, neither the Guggenheim Foundation nor the Abu Dhabi government have officially announced the closure of the project. The Guggenheim Foundation confirmed that "it remains committed to the Guggenheim Abu Dhabi and its transformative potential as a catalyst for exchange and for expanding the narratives of art history" (Ruiz 2017). At the moment, one can only speculate whether the new Guggenheim branch in Abu Dhabi will become a reality. Nevertheless, the development of the project is a good illustration of how the Guggenheim brand gained its power during the 2000s, when local authorities in different countries believed the "Bilbao effect" could be replicated.

The urban regeneration that attracted city officials to the Guggenheim brand, though, was not the only motivation driving investors to invite satellite museums to their locations. The Guggenheim, with its global presence and growing international audiences, has also become an appealing partner for transnational corporations. As the former head of the Guggenheim's Board acknowledged, with the growth of the Guggenheim brand internationally, the museum has "been successful in gaining financial support from image-conscious foreign corporations now operating in the United States" (Lawson-Johnston 2014, 136). One of the first corporate franchises developed by the museum was the Deutsche Guggenheim, opened in 1997 and closed later in 2013. It emerged as a partnership between the Guggenheim Foundation and Deutsche Bank, one of the largest corporate collectors of fine art in the world.

In the late 1970s, the bank began its Art at Work program, collecting fine art as a type of alternative financial investment. It allowed the company to promote the public good while benefiting from ever-increasing art values, as well as tax incentives (Harold 2001). By the end of the twentieth century, the bank opened hundreds of international branches in more than 75 countries. At the same time, it acquired more than 50,000 works of art. These pieces are on display in corporate offices from Frankfurt to New York to Singapore and São Paulo for the enjoyment of clients and employees (Deutsche Bank 2007).

Hilmar Kopper, then president of the bank, described the opening of the Deutsche Guggenheim as "an advertisement for Deutsche Bank's global expertise, quality, and innovative potential" (Haacke 2005, 119). Guggenheim in Berlin was opened when the Deutsche Bank sought to improve its image and reputation in the international arena. It was especially critical after the public disclosure of the Nazi file archives in 1995 in the Warsaw Pact countries (Decker 2008). The archives revealed the Deutsche Bank's direct involvement in supporting the Nazi regime that led to the genocide of millions of Jewish people in World War II. Increasingly dependent on government support for survival during World War II, Deutsche Bank spread through conquered territories, seeing them as the only remaining growth area (Gall et al. 1995; Harold 2001). With such a historical burden, the bank was looking for ways to rewrite its dark corporate history (Decker 2008). Deutsche Guggenheim provided a platform to improve their institutional brand on the world stage by associating it with the name of a globally recognised museum, and "essentially with a Jewish name," as Krens would note.

According to the partnership agreement, the Deutsche Bank committed to covering all expenses associated with the creation and maintenance of the museum galleries and exhibitions displays. From its side, the Guggenheim offered curatorial expertise and support for all exhibition and publication productions (Deutsche Guggenheim 1999). Housed in a small 510-square-meter interior gallery of the Deutsche Bank in Berlin, the museum boasted a rich program of exhibitions, including a show from the Deutsche Bank's art collections and three Guggenheim shows each year. Some of these exhibits featured distinguished international artists such as William Kentridge, Jeff Koons, Gerhard Richter and many others (Guggenheim 2013).

The museum in Berlin was a popular tourist destination. By the end of 2011, it had attracted almost 2 million visitors, with half of them being international, which "is quite a lot for such a small space" (Bernshausen 2011). Nevertheless, the Deutsche Guggenheim was closed after 15 years. Neither the bank nor the Guggenheim would explain their decision to the public, saying only that their contract expired at the end of 2012. However, the Guggenheim Foundation director Richard Armstrong hinted that "Berlin today is a very different city from what it was when we began. We feel the time is right now to step back and re-examine our collaboration" (Vogel 2012).

The official website of the KunstHalle, a new art centre established by the Deutsche Bank right after the closure of the Guggenheim branch, pointed to a drastic shift in corporate priorities in its art program, global role and mission. In contrast to the Guggenheim's commitments to promote international arts, KunstHalle put greater emphasis on its own collections and committed to support emerging German artists, "young talents on Berlin's international art scene, presenting them for the first time to a broad public" (KunstHalle 2015).

In franchise relationships with the Guggenheim, the branch in Berlin had very modest opportunities to "showcase the largest corporate collection of fine art in the world" (Deutsche Bank 2007). According to the franchise arrangements, the Deutsche Guggenheim could offer its own exhibition only once per year and "the only one independently curated by the Bank"

(Bernshausen 2011). Other exhibitions were curated from the Guggenheim in New York, limiting the exposure and promotion of local German artists. "As a private institution we believe that we should give something extra which public museums cannot do," the Deutsche Guggenheim Program Manager explained, "and at the end of the day we need to find our own niche in the global art landscape" (Bernshausen 2011).

During 15 years of running the Guggenheim franchise in Berlin, Deutsche Bank improved its corporate reputation as a global expert in art collection and curation. The closure of the Deutsche Guggenheim was evidence that the museum's brand had been temporarily acquired by the transnational corporate patron in order to rebrand its own global image (Decker 2008). Once this was achieved, Deutsche Bank did not see any reason to extend the franchise agreement with the Guggenheim, because it was clear these organisations had divergent missions in the global art world. On the one hand, the example of Deutsche Guggenheim demonstrates that the museum's brand value was rapidly growing at the beginning of the twenty-first century. Deutsche Bank temporarily committed to this franchise because it was a much faster and easier way to enhance its own brand value and global visibility.

On the other hand, this case indicates the short-term and unsustainable nature of corporate franchises. Many of these appear to be driven by immediate interests of transnational corporations, rather than by long-term commitments to develop and nurture mutually beneficial relationships. The Guggenheim–Hermitage branch in Las Vegas, in partnership with Sands Corporation, demonstrated a similar mercenary approach to museum franchising. It emerged purely as a business project when a billion-dollar corporation, the Venetian Hotel–Resort–Casino, expressed interest in opening a Guggenheim branch as a part of its grand entertainment complex.

Sheldon Adelson, the owner of the Venetian Hotel–Resort–Casino, saw a very profitable business deal in offering museum opportunities to his customers to enrich their casino experiences. "Nobody would have dreamed of a Guggenheim Las Vegas," he said. "Steve Wynn started [his first private Art Gallery] in the Bellagio Hotel and was successful. We are not ashamed to say we took a page out of his book" (Esterow 2001). In this interview, Adelson referred to the Bellagio Casino experience, where the owner Steve Wynn, a wealthy art patron with a personal collection valued at $300 million, opened the Bellagio Gallery of Fine Art in 1998.

The business success of Wynn's venture was self-explanatory. The gallery attracted 15,000 visitors daily, paying a $12 entry fee (Bellagio Gallery of Fine Art 2005). Such attendance convinced both Adelson and Krens that a Guggenheim branch would be worthwhile in a city that receives millions of tourists each day. "We have been impressed at the size of the audience and the degree of attention of visitors at the Bellagio," Krens confirmed (Esterow 2001).

Around that time, Hermitage Museum Director Mikhail Piotrovsky contacted Krens to discuss a potential partnership. Piotrovsky was actively search for more sustainable funding sources for the museum outside Russia. Both museums had world-recognised collections, institutional expertise and global recognition. And they were both interested in expanding their exhibition spaces to attract more visitors and investments (Trilupaityte 2009, 125). The Venetian Hotel–Resort–Casino proposal offered both museums what they were looking for – corporate investment, a space for new exhibitions in a new geographic location and quite promising visitor projections (Rymer 2000).

As a result, in 2001, Krens, Piotrovsky and Adelson signed a contract to develop a Guggenheim–Hermitage Las Vegas. It was hosted in a newly constructed building located in the lobby of the Venetian Hotel–Resort–Casino to house major works from both institutions (Varoli 2000). The Las Vegas Sands Corporation invested $30 million to build the museum. It also contributed $8.6 million as start-up capital and agreed to pay a licence fee of $10 million per year to the Guggenheim (Rosenbaum 2003). Despite the promising projections for audience development, the joint exhibitions of the Guggenheim–Hermitage in Las Vegas did not attract the expected number of visitors. Actual attendance hardly exceeded a thousand visitors on any given day (Hansen and Rogers 2003).

Apart from the opening exhibition, which brought the famous "Art of Motorcycles" show from New York, the Las Vegas branch exercised a more conservative curatorial approach. Guggenheim–Hermitage exhibited masterpieces from world-recognised artists such as Picasso, Renoir, Cezanne and Kandinsky, which perhaps did not give the Las Vegas audience the grand spectacle they were looking for (Hansen and Rogers 2003).

In January 2003, the Guggenheim–Hermitage Las Vegas closed. Krens and Piotrovsky could not sustain the financial costs of bringing new exhibitions to the museum. Adelson – who failed to gain returns on his investments – quickly lost interest in the whole project. He found more profitable ways of using the museum space in the lobby of the Venetian Hotel–Resort–Casino by converting the museum into a theatre for stage shows (Muschamp 2002). Despite the closure of the museum, however, Adelson and the Las Vegas Sands Corporation continued to officially promote their partnership with Guggenheim and Hermitage, producing an impression that the museum might reopen in future (Decker 2008).

In 2005, the Las Vegas Sands Corporation participated in a bid for a $3.2 billion plan to develop the 50-acre West Kowloon Cultural District in Hong Kong, for which it sought approval from the Hong Kong government. The urban development proposal required strong affiliations with cultural institutions to convince regional and federal governments that the company had sufficient expertise in urban cultural regeneration. The Guggenheim–Hermitage satellite in Las Vegas helped the Las Vegas Sands Corporation to

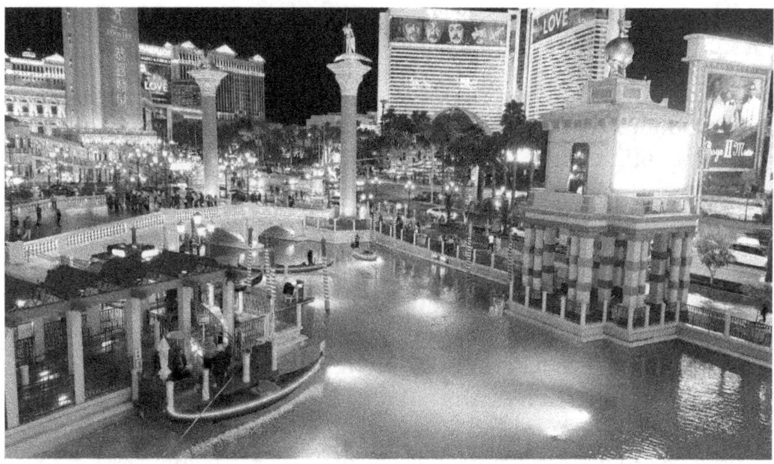

Figure 3.3 Venetian Hotel–Resort–Casino, Las Vegas (USA)

Source: "The Venetian" by Jim Twitchell, www.flickr.com/photos/redacted/32907553735/ Licence at https://creativecommons.org/licenses/by-sa//2.0/

negotiate with the Hong Kong government (Decker 2008). Quite logically, after receiving the preliminary approval for their proposal in 2007, the affiliation with both museums was no longer necessary. It led to the official closure of the franchise agreement (Peterson 2008) and the entire Guggenheim–Hermitage project was finally cancelled in 2008 (Fabelová 2010).

The failure of the project also suggested that the key drivers behind the Las Vegas branch were economic interests and agenda in corporate brand development on the global stage.

In both cases, Deutsche Guggenheim and Guggenheim–Hermitage in Las Vegas, the corporate partners aimed to boost their global recognition as powerful art patrons to achieve their institutional interests. By associating their names with the Guggenheim brand, both corporations sought to project more appealing images while entering new markets in pursuit of their economic goals. Even though both projects were eventually closed, the examples illuminate the power and value of the Guggenheim's reputation in the global arena.

Indeed, in the early 2000s the Guggenheim brand kept attracting local authorities and transnational corporations to invest in multimillion-dollar projects to develop new branches in different countries. The franchise made "Guggenheim the most attractive museum for global capital." It was "marketed across the world from Wall Street/Manhattan, even becoming subject to a McDonaldized rationality" (Zulaika 2001, 112). Not surprisingly, the franchise idea started to receive more criticism in media and academia, while new failures of Guggenheim branches generated more controversies and concerns among local communities.

Guggenheim franchises: McDonaldised practices on decline

The Guggenheim franchising practices have, in many cases, been surrounded by controversy – especially those failed projects that enthusiastically started in different parts of the world but eventually closed down. The Guggenheim Rio is a classic unsuccessful deal. It illustrates strong tension between a local government's economic regeneration agenda and taxpayers' concerns about the feasibility and cultural value of such a project. The museum in Rio was to be built on Brazil's Guanabara Bay and designed by the famous French architect, Jean Nouvel, to boost tourism in the city (Celso 2001).

In 2003, Krens and the then-mayor of Rio de Janeiro, Cesar Ricardo Macieira, signed an agreement for the city government to fully finance the construction of the new Guggenheim Museum branch in Rio. According to the contract, the government agreed to cover all operational costs, including $11 million in construction, as well as $28.6 million in franchise fees to the Guggenheim Foundation (Kaufman 2003, 6). However, that same year saw the election of a new left-wing president, Luiz Ignacio Lula da Silva, causing markets to panic. This led to losses in Brazil's national currency of about one-third of its value against the U.S. dollar and triggered high inflation (Rosenbaum 2003, 46). This economic instability raised concerns among the local public about the Rio government's capacity to fund the expensive project with Guggenheim.

Members of the Rio community and new left-wing civil society groups actively protested the initiative, pointing out that the amount of funding allocated for the new museum could have been invested in local development. For example, "the enormous outlay to build the museum could pave 3,500 kilometers of roads or construct 6,000 schools, 7,500 day-care centers, or 4,000 health clinics" (Kaufman 2003, 6). The Rio government tried to justify its plans, referring to the earlier-conducted feasibility study. It predicted annual attendance to the site to exceed a million visitors. Not only did this high volume of visitors promise to return investments in only four years, it projected a high site-generated income of $500 million to be reached every year (Vogel 2003).

Despite such positive economic projections, the Brazilian artistic community saw the project in terms of the global forces of neo-colonisation exercised by Guggenheim. "The winner in this business is the Guggenheim, and the losers are all the Brazilian institutions," argued Isabella Prata, former Director of the Museum of Modern Art of São Paulo. "We're still acting like some

Indians open to exploitation by a new set of colonizers [. . .] Wouldn't it be better to invest in Brazilian institutions?" (Celso 2001). In January 2004, after a formal investigation into the project, the national court blocked the Guggenheim contract and deemed it illegal (Kaufman 2004, 14). This led to the official cancellation of the project by the mayor of Rio de Janeiro in 2005.

Among more recent unsuccessful projects are European attempts to establish Guggenheim–Hermitage Vilnius (2008) and then Guggenheim Helsinki (2011). In both cases, similar to the Brazilian experience, the projects were strongly supported by their local city authorities and private investors. New branches were envisioned as a way to address economic downturns and to improve city economies by boosting tourism through cultural regeneration. However, both projects faced a strong resistance from the "populist far right" and members of the Left and Social Democrats protesting against investing taxpayers' money into an enormously expensive private institution from the U.S. After several unsuccessful attempts to reignite the project in Vilnius, the Guggenheim Museum's initiative was finally taken to Helsinki, Finland (Radzevicius 2011).

Despite the fact that one-third of the fundraising target had been pledged in support of the $138 million Guggenheim Helsinki project, in early 2016 Finnish city lawmakers eventually voted the project down (Siegal 2016). The main stakeholders of the project argued that it was strongly supported by the local business community. For example, Ari Lahti, an investment banker and Chairman of Guggenheim Helsinki, said: "We have received donations, with no strings attached, from the hotels in Finland; restaurants in Helsinki; Finnair, the national airline company; the three big ferry companies that operate in Helsinki" (Siegal 2016). However, the project failed to garner support from residents and the artistic community, who were reluctant to welcome "starchitect supermarket" or "the cultural equivalent of Starbucks" to their city (Goff 2017). "We are not paying taxes to be handed over to an American corporation," public voices in the heated debate declared. "If we're spending that kind of money, it should be on our own national museum, not another outpost of a global company" (Wainwright 2014).

In the academic scholarship, the Guggenheim's franchise practices were also criticised for damaging local artistic ecologies through cultural homogenisation. When a city government invited the Guggenheim satellites to their urban location, critics would argue, they "undersell their own cultural identity," while trying to project "modernity, internationalism, and maturity" (Dolan 1999, 60). For example, dedicated researchers of Guggenheim Bilbao specifically pointed out the "absence of local artists" in the museum's permanent collections and exhibitions. By contrast, Guggenheim Bilbao's acquisitions include art pieces by Anselm Kiefer, Andy Warhol, Richard Serra, Mark Rothko, Jones Rosenquist, Robert Rauschenberg, Jeff Koons, Louise Bourgeous and many other American artists (Plaza et al. 2009)

No matter who owns a Guggenheim branch, the New York-based Foundation oversees the collections, curatorial activities, programming and marketing across all museums carrying its brand (Mathur 2005, 670). By embracing the "Guggenheim concept," museum scholars stressed, local communities "disconnect from their geography" and promote "particular globally oriented ideology" (Rauen 2001, 296). In critical scholarship, this ideology was directly associated with American cultural imperialism: "Branding is the medium of empire" (Sorkin 2005, 31). French art historian Jean Ciair said:

> Just as an Empire, continuously expanding its borders, ends up forgetting its center, and the center ends up no longer knowing its limits, so too the Museum [. . .] ends up forgetting, if not betraying, that for which it was created.
>
> (Newhouse 1998, 66)

In response to the criticism, Krens would say: "Those who call us that [McGuggenheim] have no idea. Do we have the same façade, the same emblem, the same contents everywhere? No. We have established a local accent everywhere" (Knöfel and von Dewitz 2008). He always emphasised that the network reflects the museum's "commitment to international communication and global cultural exchange," and that "the Guggenheim implicitly regards all contemporary cultures and their traditions as potential partners" (Guggenheim 2006). One of the Guggenheim Board members from Bilbao, Jon Azua, also stressed that the global network allows the museum to develop "better exhibitions, [. . .] attracts more and better artists and collections, [. . .] and contributes to enhancing better relationships between different countries, regions, cultures, and people" (Azua 2005, 83).

This inspirational rhetoric, claiming that the global cultural exchange is the Guggenheim's key priority in the franchise model, points to the museum's ambition to play an important role in building bridges of cross-cultural communication to improve international relations. The question is, though, what these franchise practices can really offer to enhance international relations and whether they can complement cultural diplomacy. Arguably, Krens's potential franchising deals around the world pushed the Guggenheim to reinforce its international exchanges with, and presence in, various countries of strategic interest. For instance, in relation to the Rio branch, Krens pointed out: "North America doesn't take South American art seriously enough. We wanted to change that" (Knöfel and von Dewitz 2008).

Indeed, during negotiations with the Brazilian government to build a new satellite museum in Rio, Krens toured the Brazilian art exhibition "Brazil: Body and Soul." It was first housed in the New York museum in 2001 and then travelled to the Bilbao branch the following year. The exhibition featured works from the seventeenth and eighteenth centuries, along with modern and contemporary art to explore cultural diversity of Brazilian artistic expression (Guggenheim 2002). However, by organising such an exhibition, Guggenheim intended to appeal to the Brazilian community. The exhibition featuring Brazilian art helped Krens to negotiate a deal with local authorities in Rio by projecting a positive image of Guggenheim in the eyes of foreign publics (Decker 2008).

A similar brand strategy was employed in earlier travelling exhibitions, such as "Masterworks from the Guggenheim." Between 1990 and 1992, a series of these exhibitions visited places under consideration for satellite museums, including Madrid, Tokyo, Sydney and Montreal (Decker 2008). Claiming to develop international cultural relations with museums and cultural institutions from other countries, these exhibits served as important initiatives that furthered the Guggenheim's plans for global expansion by entering new cultural markets. In the same way as the case of global corporatisation initiatives, museum franchising in the context of the Guggenheim was mainly employed by Krens as a business idea that served the economic goals of involved stakeholders.

In the last decade, despite strong criticism, the Guggenheim franchise idea has remained quite appealing to potential international investors seeking institutional rebranding or cultural regeneration. In 2014, the Director of the Guggenheim, Richard Armstrong, commented: "it's a rare week when [he] doesn't receive at least one request to build a museum somewhere in the world" (Wise 2014). But after Krens left the Guggenheim in 2008, the new leadership drastically shifted the focus and priorities in the museum's global expansion agenda. In contrast to Krens, Armstrong intended "to have a significant impact in the world without having to build a building" (Lund and Greyser 2015, 12). The new Guggenheim's director openly shared his vision with the media: "We don't engage with a very high proportion of people, and the possibility of going on ad infinitum is really not attractive" (Wise 2014).

Specifically, Armstrong emphasised that Guggenheim needed "to stop being an exporting institution and instead be a collaborative one" (Rosenbaum 2014). In pursuit of higher economic returns, the Guggenheim, under Krens, failed to realise the potential of museum franchising to establish long-term collaborative cultural relations across countries and communities. A number of unsuccessful projects and closed branches in different countries provide good evidence. This task, however, was excellently implemented by the State Hermitage Museum in Russia.

As discussed earlier, the Hermitage partnered with the Guggenheim in several franchise projects and, initially, was also driven by strong economic interests. In contrast to the Guggenheim branches, though, the Hermitage International Network is thriving and rapidly growing across countries and continents, while developing strong connections with local communities. Furthermore, unlike the Guggenheim franchise strategy, it is also a political project that opens new channels for cultural diplomacy in Russia. In the following sections, the chapter will explore the evolution of museum franchising into a new form of non-state diplomacy in the context of authoritarian Russia.

Re-birth of the museum franchise in authoritarian Russia

After the collapse of the Soviet Empire in the 1990s, the rapidly declining reputation of Russia as a strong military power and an authority in scientific endeavour urged the new government to improve its image on the world stage. During his first presidency, Putin repeatedly referred to the "Russian civilisation" of internationally recognised writers, musicians and artists as main sources of the country's appeal in the eyes of the foreign publics (Wilson 2015, 294).

In the 2000s, the federal government prioritised its support for major national cultural intuitions that, throughout Russian history, had played a key role in projecting a powerful image of the country in the international arena. For example, in 2011, $760 million in renovations were completed at the Bolshoi Theatre, which was a major player in Cold War dance diplomacy by means of taking this famous Russian ballet on international tours (Prevots 2001). The Bolshoi Ballet and Bolshoi Opera are the oldest, largest and most renowned ballet and opera companies in the world. The legacy of the Bolshoi Theatre goes back to eighteenth-century imperial Russia, when it was established in 1776 under the rule of Catherine the Great.

The State Hermitage Museum in Saint Petersburg stands out as one of the most important cultural players in the world of visual arts in Russia and is of the same, if not a bigger, calibre. The museum is well recognised globally for its rich and diverse collections, which include Buddhist frescoes, Islamic and Oriental artefacts, Roman and Greek antiquities, Scythian and Greek gold and works of European artists such as Rembrandt, Leonardo da Vinci, Matisse and Rubens (Piotrovsky 2003). Since its inception by Catherine the Great in 1764, the Hermitage took a leading role in representing Russian history, culture and heritage to the world.

For example, Emperor Nicholas I strategically used Hermitage exhibitions in the mid-nineteenth century to display and assert a greater role for an emergent Russia in the European state system (Digout 2006). During the Soviet Empire, the museum was heavily employed as a vehicle of communist propaganda. Throughout the Cold War, the State Hermitage Museum's international tours and exhibitions abroad were directly commissioned and initiated by the Russian government. Vitali Suslov, who has worked at the Hermitage since 1967 and is one of the most renowned museum professionals in Russia, once said: "We would get a telegram or telephone call from Kremlin saying it would be very good if you could arrange an exhibition in London, France or America . . . The next week it would be somewhere different" (Norman 2005, 311).

In most cases, these projects were directly associated with a state visit, and the exhibitions abroad were formally opened by presidents, prime ministers or other high-level political figures in different corners of the world. In almost every country, an exhibition of the Shishkin and Morozov, the most famous "Russian genre" painters, was on display to showcase the beauty

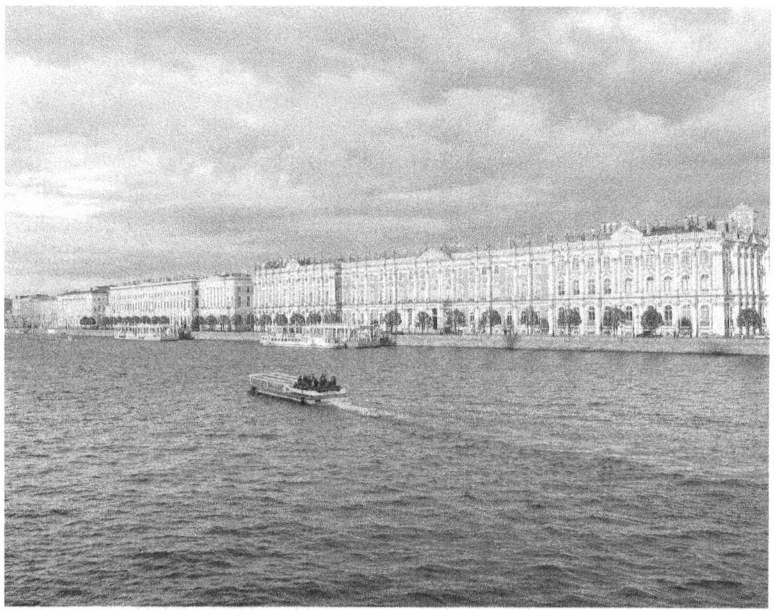

Figure 3.4 The State Hermitage Museum, the view from the Neva River, Saint Petersburg (Russia)

Source: "Hermitage, St. Petersburg" by cdschock, www.flickr.com/photos/chrisandlori/10639239674 Licence at https://creativecommons.org/licenses/by-sa//2.0/

and romanticism of Russian landscape and life (Norman 2005). In terms of museum leadership, the previous and the current directors of the Hermitage, Boris Piotrovsky and his son Mikhail Piotrovsky, were directly appointed by the Russian government, but "for diametrically opposite reasons":

> Boris Piotrovsky, who joined the Communist Party in 1945, was selected as a safe man for the job at the opening of the repressive Brezhnev era, while his son Mikhail was appointed [. . .] because he was a dynamic, cosmopolitan scholar who looked capable of steering the museum through the rough water of perestroika.
>
> (Norman 2005, 304)

Following the long-established tradition of sustaining close ties with the government, the State Hermitage Museum remains one of the central national cultural institutions playing the leading role in the high-level political and diplomatic life of Russia. In the recent decades, Putin has utilised the Hermitage galleries as hosting spaces for numerous diplomatic high-level meetings. These have included visits by the Dutch Prime Minister Mark Rutte, Korean President Park Geun-hye, German Chancellor Angela Merkel and UNESCO Director General Irina Bokova, to name just a few. By decree of the President of the Russian Federation, the State Hermitage Museum was designated as a part of the National Heritage of the people of Russia.

Indeed, the State Hermitage Museum in Saint Petersburg is more than just a museum. It is arguably the most important cultural institution in Russia and enjoys a privileged position among other institutions in the country. It is the only museum that functions under the special patronage of the President of the Russian Federation. It also has its own line in the federal budget of Russia and receives 83 per cent of its funding directly from the Russian government – not through the Ministry of Culture. This government money takes the form of annual subsidies, including 23 per cent of funds allocated for implementing the government's national and foreign policies (State Hermitage Museum 2010–2014).

The Director of the Hermitage, Piotrovsky, enjoys a special personal relationship with the president of Russia, Vladimir Putin. At the beginning of his career, Putin served as Deputy Head within Saint Petersburg's city administration, with specific responsibility for foreign relations. During this time, he became quite familiar with the Hermitage's governance, projects and international activities (Hoyle 2014). In a number of interviews, Piotrovsky shared that Putin is very knowledgeable about the Hermitage, and over the years they have developed a strong connection (Kishkovsky 2009).

The Hermitage's leading position among Russian cultural institutions is also reinforced through direct connections with national media and broadcasting agencies. For example, the Russian national and regional television channels have developed a longstanding close collaboration with the museum on different series of programs, including *My Hermitage* on the national TV channel, and *Culture* and *The Treasures of St Petersburg* on Saint Petersburg regional television. In developing further regional links, the Hermitage cycle of television programs has now been broadcast on dozens of channels "from Kaliningrad in the west to Sakhalin in the east" (Matveev 2003, 69).

Additionally, in recent years, the museum has garnered even greater support for its expansion programs from Russia's government. The government not only granted the Hermitage a large historical building located nearby – the General Staff Building, one of the most famous architectural monuments in Saint Petersburg, designed by K. I. Rossi and built in 1830 – but Putin and Piotrovsky also announced further plans to launch several new Hermitage satellite museums in provincial areas throughout Russia in the cities of Vladivostok, Yekaterinburg, Omsk and Kaluga.

In 2005, the State Hermitage opened its satellite branch – the Hermitage–Kazan Exhibition Centre in the city of Kazan. It was established with the patronage and support of the president of the Republic of Tatarstan,

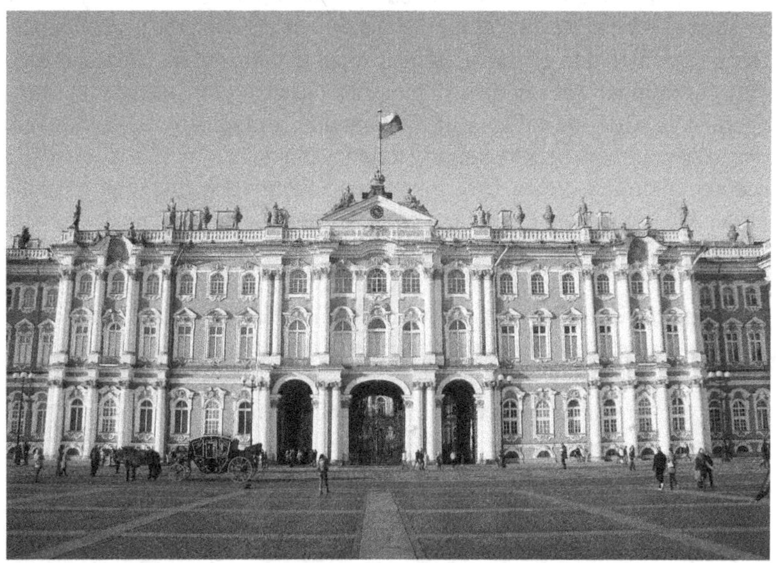

Figure 3.5 The State Hermitage Museum, Saint Petersburg (Russia)

Source: "Winter Palace Facade" by Jamesn www.flickr.com/photos/-jamesn-/8343402144/ Licence at https://creativecommons.org/licenses/by-sa//2.0/

Mintimer Shaimiyev. A subdivision of the State Historical, Architectural and National Art Museum–Reserve, the satellite museum is situated on the site of the Kazan Kremlin to facilitate international cultural relations between Russia, Kazan and the Middle East (State Hermitage Museum 2005). In this regard, the development of the International Network of the Hermitage Museum Foundations in the Netherlands, U.S., U.K., Canada, Israel, Finland and Italy seems like a political project with significant involvement from the Russian government.

Indeed, the Hermitage Foundations abroad are official sites of major international political and cultural events, serving as dedicated spaces for diplomatic exchanges, elite meetings and international cultural celebrations. For example, in 2007, the Hermitage–Italy Centre in Ferrara, fully funded by the Italian city government and private contributors, was opened in the presence of the president of Italy, Giorgio Napolitano (State Hermitage Museum 2007). Acknowledging the political significance of this international expansion, Piotrovsky indicated that the International Hermitage Network is, to a certain extent, a diplomatic project with a mission to improve cultural ties and collaborative cultural relations between Russia and the rest of the world (Piotrovsky 2017a).

However, the project was not initiated by the Russian government and was not supported or commissioned by it. Instead, as the history of the museum demonstrates, it was born in conditions of economic necessity. The Hermitage started to solicit additional support from abroad when the Russian government was not able to maintain the high costs of the museum's operations. After the collapse of the communist regime in the 1990s, federal support from the Russian government plummeted due to devastating economic turmoil. When Director Mikhail Piotrovsky, first took over the leadership of the State Hermitage in 1990, the museum was threatened with closure. The government at that time had announced it would only pay two-thirds of museum salaries and refused to pay old debts accumulated during the economic instability of the perestroika era (Norman 2005).

Furthermore, the philanthropic tradition in Russian society was destroyed after the revolution in 1917, and it presented a challenging environment to secure meaningful support from the new economic elite in Russia. A revolutionary change came to the Hermitage with Mikhail Piotrovsky, who established a worldwide network of foundations to solicit funding from international sources. As the director himself explained, the museum's global ventures and the Greater Hermitage Project were born out of necessity: "Our big activities and conceptions were born in conditions of crisis" (Kishkovsky 2009). This network provided a reliable and "solid base of financial assistance to the museum," making possible a number of long-term, expensive projects, including the restoration of museum halls,

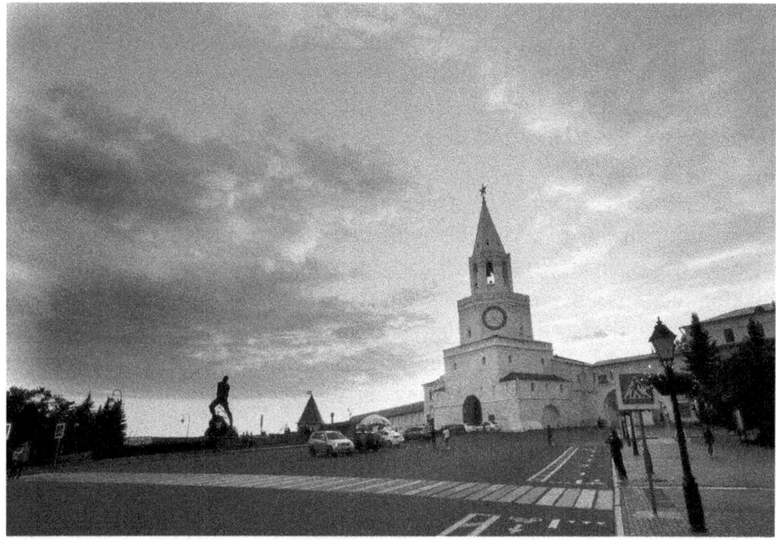

Figure 3.6 Kazan Kremlin State Historical and Architectural Museum–Reserve, the host space of the Hermitage–Kazan Exhibition Centre

Source: "Kazan Kremlin, sundown" by John Perry www.flickr.com/photos/cantanima/42236730594/ Licence at https://creativecommons.org/licenses/by-sa//2.0/

improvement of visitor access and the acquisition of new collections and exhibitions (State Hermitage Museum 2017a).

For example, a major fundraising campaign was organised by the Hermitage Foundation in the Netherlands during a touring exhibition from Saint Petersburg entitled "Catherine the Great, the Emperor, and the Arts." As a result of this project, the Foundation gathered enough funds from private sources to successfully complete a major restoration project – New Roof and New Lighting for Rembrandt (1998) (State Hermitage Museum 2017a). Moreover, the opening of its first satellite museum in Europe, the Hermitage Amsterdam, in 2004 not only provided new exhibition spaces outside of Russia but also offered new sources of revenue at a time the museum "was facing both a surplus of deferred maintenance projects and a lack of funds." The Amsterdam branch raises funds for the State Hermitage through ticket sales, allocating one euro per visitor in Amsterdam to contribute to the museum in Russia (Tromp 2009, 202).

Although the International Network's ultimate aim was generating revenue, the management of the museum recognised that raising support was intimately tied to establishing strong and long-lasting connections with foreign constituencies (Gibson 2003). The strategic development of the network was based on building strong connections with local communities. As Piotrovsky explained, opening a new branch abroad is a very time-consuming process and "should be treated very carefully. Any haste will lead to just usual outward appearance, which then fails. It is important that in the place where you plan to open a Hermitage center, there is a permanent interest" (Mamaeva 2017).

The Hermitage approach to international franchising has been based on creating strong relationships with international partners "in the form of expertise exchanges" or "scholarly exchange and exhibitions aimed at making the museum's collections and staff more accessible to the international community" (Gibson 2003, 22). This commitment to cross-cultural exchange, collaborations and nurturing mutually beneficial relationships was instrumental in engaging new audiences and communities across countries. It also led to the opening of new avenues for cultural diplomacy beyond the control of the Russian government.

Founded as independent non-profit organisations abroad, the Hermitage Foundations across continents operate within their national contexts and act in accordance with the legislation of the non-profit management of their respective countries (Sirakanian 2017). The "foreign status" of the Foundations, as the Head of the Development Department explained, is a great advantage. It allows the museums to consolidate cultural and economic resources from local communities overseas and attract not only international funding, but also expertise and ideas, facilitating a genuine cultural exchange (Sirakanian 2017). Run by national representatives, these foundations are fully funded and supported by foreign stakeholders and local communities. Nonetheless, they promote Russian language, history and legacy overseas and establish bilateral relationships with local cultural institutions and audiences. These activities, whether intentional or not, contribute to the foreign policy objectives of Russia without direct or indirect support, commission or patronage from the Russian government.

Hermitage goes global: contributing to cultural diplomacy of Russia

The Hermitage global networking approach draws on the resources, funds and expertise of international civil society, private patrons and stakeholders from abroad. The Head of the Development Department at the State Hermitage Museum pointed out that, in most cases, the main initiative for developing new Foundation branches comes from influential people and organisations abroad, and never from the Hermitage itself (Sirakanian 2017). One of the strengths of the Hermitage has been its focus on Russian diaspora communities. All Foundations within the network offer a rich and diverse program for community engagement. These programs usually attract immigrants and expatriates from Russia while connecting them back to their national heritage to celebrate native language, culture and history.

Importantly, these events strongly rely on organisational help from volunteers and community leaders, and most of them are of Russian origin. For example, the Hermitage Museum Foundation USA receives remarkable support from the Russian nobility, or so-called white Russians descended from noble families who supported the Russian Empire and escaped the country after the Revolution in 1917. One such member of the Russian noble diaspora is Masha Tolstoy Sarandinaki, the American-born great-granddaughter of the famous Russian writer Leo Tolstoy. Her grandfather, Vladimir Tolstoy, escaped from Russia in 1919 during the Bolshevik Revolution and moved from Paris to New York in 1949 (Ilienko-Chung 2014).

For many years, Tolstoy Sarandinaki served the U.S. Foundation as CEO, contributing to the foundation's activities with her energy and loyalty to Russian cultural heritage and her family legacy. Only in 2000, when Tolstoy Sarandinaki was 49 years of age, did she finally visit her great-grandfather's country home, Yasnaya Polyana, to reunite with 300 other Tolstoy descendants from all over the world (Ilienko-Chung 2014). She now goes to Saint Petersburg every year, not only to visit Yasnaya Polyana, but also to attend the Hermitage Gala, one of the most important annual fundraising events at which the museum celebrates the continued support from the members of its International Network of Foundations. "This magnificent celebration, worthy of the Russian Tsars," usually has a rich program of special exhibitions (State Hermitage Museum 2017b). They include concerts by opera and ballet stars in the Hermitage galleries and the traditional ball in the Winter Palace, attracting wealthy donors from abroad (State Hermitage Museum 2017b).

The Russian diaspora provides the Hermitage museum with strong international support through human resources, in-kind help and cash donations, as well as direct contributions to numerous development programs. Nurturing and bonding with the Russian diaspora in different countries has been shown to work well in creating a favourable environment for cultural exchanges, with strong implications for diplomacy. Drawing on my personal experience in serving the U.S. Foundation as an event coordinator in the Washington DC area in 2010, I can share the following example. It demonstrates how the Foundation's events function as sites of public mobilisation. These events exclusively draw on the enthusiasm and commitment of the diaspora community, but eventually they become places of official cultural diplomacy.

In June 2010, I initiated and helped organise a reception and screening of *The Hermitage Dwellers* in Washington DC. It is a documentary about the museum by the Dutch filmmaker Aliona Van Der Horst. Located primarily in New York, the U.S. Foundation does not have its own venue in Washington. In pursuit of expanding its networks and community, Paul Rodzianko, then Chair of the Hermitage Foundation in the U.S., invited me to be a part of the organisation to serve as the only event coordinator located outside New York. Excited to bring the Hermitage programs to the capital area, I was enthusiastic about starting a preparation campaign for this event. This included securing a suitable venue, soliciting funding to cover organisational costs for the screening and a reception with drinks and refreshments, as well as marketing and promotional activities. This was not an easy task for a single volunteer located in a different city.

Help came from the Russian diaspora community. Eventually, the event was hosted by the Russian Cultural Centre – a subordinate of the Russian Federal Agency for the Commonwealth of Independent States, Compatriots Living Abroad and International Humanitarian Cooperation. Created as a bilateral agreement between the United States and Russia in 1985 "to develop and maintain positive relations between the Russian and American people" (Russian Cultural Centre 2017), the centre served as a perfect venue. The Russian Cultural Centre not only provided in-kind support for the film screening but also facilitated connections with its large audiences and Russian political elites in the capital area.

The screening attracted many people from the local community and not only Russian immigrants. Dr Viacheslav Moshkalo, Russian Cultural Attaché to the USA, welcomed the assembled guests and the Foundation to the home of Russian culture in the capital city. The event was organised with the help of new volunteers from the local Russian student community, including Anastasia Koshkina and Tatiana Blinkova, graduate students at American University (Grincheva 2010). The reception and film screening were one of the first fruitful public events organised outside New York. It allowed the Foundation to reach out to new audiences and promote its existence among potential new patrons.

This story is particularly illustrative as it demonstrates that in drawing on the support of people who share multiple identities, both Russian and those associated with their countries of residencies, the Hermitage network significantly contributes to the Russian government's foreign policy objectives. Specifically, events such as the documentary screening, as well as many other exhibitions, book launches, artistic workshops and community celebrations organised by foundations from Europe to North America, help "to consolidate the Russian-speaking diaspora" abroad (MFARF 2016). Recognised as a priority in Russian public diplomacy, this engagement with Russian compatriots aims to strengthen international person-to-person relationships to improve the reputation of the country among foreign publics (RPDS 2017).

The Hermitage Foundations, though, not only are the result of efforts on behalf of Russian immigrants and expatriates of different generations but also draw on the support and genuine commitment of foreign stakeholders with shared cultural interests and missions. A good illustration is the Foundation of the Hermitage Friends in the Netherlands, which is "the largest of the existing Hermitage Friends' organizations" and the most successful (State Hermitage Museum 2017c). This foundation stresses its commitments to "share with the museum its responsibility for preserving the collections of the Dutch masters for future generations" (State Hermitage Museum 2017c). This mission reveals the very close ties between the Russian and Dutch art communities, which have evolved out of the various art exchanges that took place in previous centuries.

In fact, the Hermitage Friends in the Netherlands is the only foundation in the network that has, so far, been successful in establishing a Hermitage branch abroad. In 2004, the museum opened its first satellite museum in Europe. The Hermitage Amsterdam is a $59 million flagship project, fully supported by the Dutch lottery, the city of Amsterdam and the surrounding province of North Holland (Smale 2009). As "one of the most advanced cultural and exhibition complexes in the Netherlands" (Hermitage Amsterdam 2017), it hosts numerous travelling exhibitions organised by the Hermitage and provides a meeting space for the dedicated members of the Foundation, who engage with more than 5,000 people annually (State Hermitage Museum 2010–2014). Since its inception, the Hermitage Amsterdam has played a particularly important role in maintaining and strengthening official diplomatic ties.

The Russia Gallery, which is frequently referred to as an "embassy" and "ambassador" of Russia's national museum, is solely dedicated to the museum's origins and traces strong connections between the countries all the way back to 1697 (Goff 2017). For the Founding Director of the Hermitage Amsterdam, Ernst Veen, the museum is an agent of cultural diplomacy.

> I am a product of the Cold War. Here and now I want to make a nice exhibition. But, at the same time I also want our institution to make a small contribution to open political relations between Russia and the Netherlands.
>
> (Tromp 2009, 2017)

For example, in 2013, for the celebration of 200 years of cultural relations between the Netherlands and Russia, the museum hosted the dedicated exhibition "Peter the Great. An Inspired Tsar" and served as the main meeting space for negotiations between Vladimir Putin with King Willem Alexander and Queen Beatrix.

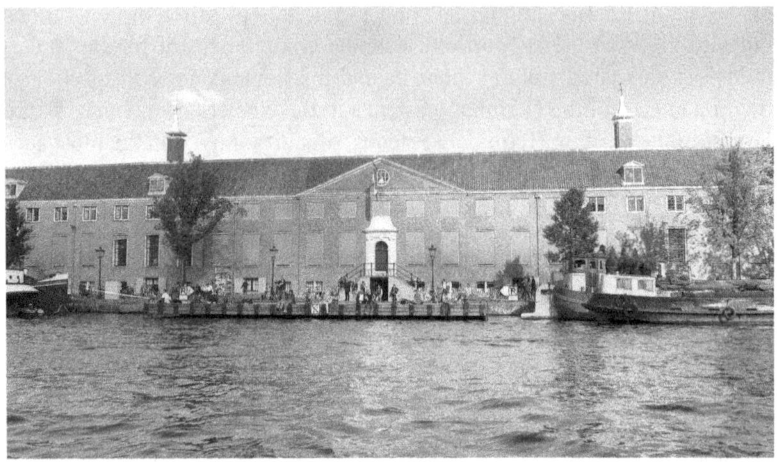

Figure 3.7 The Hermitage Amsterdam (The Netherlands)

Source: "Pays-Bas, Amsterdam, Amstelhof construit en 1682, et abritant aujourd'hui l'Hermitage d'Amsterdam" by Marie Thérèse Hébert www.flickr.com/photos/jrthibault/25806219783/ Licence at https://creativecommons.org/licenses/by-sa//2.0/

While the Russian political elite utilises Hermitage Amsterdam as an official site of cultural diplomacy, neither the Hermitage nor the Russian government initiated the opening of the branch in the Netherlands. Instead, the leadership for this project came from Ernst Veen, Chairman of the Hermitage Foundation in Amsterdam. He convinced the city government that the best creative use of the heritage building, centrally located on the Amstel River, would be to open a Hermitage branch (Goff 2017).

The network diplomacy facilitated by the Netherlands Foundation, as well as other centres across countries, is more productive than official programs of cultural diplomacy from the Russian government. An integral part of these foreign communities, the Hermitage outposts abroad do not ignite controversy or negative perceptions, in contrast to state-funded international cultural activities of the Russian government. Instead, the network's programming and events generate a strong interest among local publics in different countries, bringing in new and engaging loyal audiences. Even though all Foundations consult the Hermitage in Russia for such questions as developing exhibitions, building new audiences or attracting support (Sirakanian 2017), in fact, they are based on people-to-people exchanges that go far beyond mere promotional activities.

Various programs across Foundations in different countries reflect specific cultural needs, traditions and public appetites in their locations. These activities usually provide interested individuals with an opportunity to explore each other's cultures, either by visiting Russia or hosting events in their respected communities. For example, the State Hermitage Museum Foundation of Canada has been successful in organising an annual Hermitage Young Artists program. This program brings the most talented art students from three of Canada's leading university art schools to attend an "Art Semester" at the Hermitage, organised by the Hermitage Youth Education Centre. Through participating in this scheme, young Canadian artists develop their artistic skills by working with world-renowned Russian masters and art educators affiliated with the Hermitage (State Hermitage Museum 2010).

By contrast, the Hermitage Foundation (U.K.) hosts its unique Visiting Curators program, which brings a diverse range of specialists from different departments of the Hermitage to London to work with museum professionals from the British museums. For instance, Anna Trofimova, the Head of the Greek and Roman Department at the Hermitage, collaborated with London's libraries to develop the exhibition "Alexander the Great: The Road to the East," which was exhibited at the Hermitage, the Hermitage Amsterdam and in Australia. Another Russian curator, Lisa Renne, worked with a number of museums in London to produce a full catalogue of the British paintings from the sixteenth to nineteenth centuries in the Hermitage collections (Hermitage Museum Foundation UK 2017).

In the U.S., the Art from America program was designed by the U.S. Foundation to expand the Hermitage holdings into the twenty-first century. It allows the museum to acquire and display the works of contemporary American artists at its new exhibition spaces dedicated to modern and contemporary art. This program has been supported through a wide variety of contributions to the Hermitage collection acquisition program, which has focused on completing "that missing history of certain major global American artists" (Hermitage Museum Foundation USA 2017). For instance, in 2014, in honour of the 250th anniversary of the Hermitage, American art historian, gallery owner and art collector Helen Drutt English gifted the museum a collection of modern art totalling 74 works worth $2 million (Baigarova 2014). This program, as Piotrovsky has highlighted, stands as "a great example of the Foundation's success" in contributing to the "incredible acquisitions and works" that "show American art in all of its varieties" (Piotrovsky 2017b).

The network or franchise diplomacy of the Hermitage is more productive and enduring than official Russian government efforts in projecting soft power. Numerous activities implemented by the International Network of Foundations have positive cultural impacts on both sides and are not affected by a dynamic and unstable political climate. For example, despite the "mercy of the geopolitics" in 2014, in the context of a growing deterioration in the political relationships between Russia and the U.S., the U.S. Foundation was able to successfully implement numerous programs. They included several "White Nights" tours, four major award dinners celebrating Russian and American artists, two major international exhibitions and launches of the Art from America and Art without Borders initiatives as well as multimillion donation programs to celebrate the 250th anniversary of the Hermitage. As former Chairman of the Foundation Paul Rodzianko explained:

> Let us remember that Russia matters very much to us and that Russia is not going away. Neither is America. So: how best to understand each other? Exchanges, apolitical interaction, and tourism, of course, but we also need to maintain a national American commitment to study Russian language, Russian history and Russian culture.
>
> (Hermitage Museum Foundation USA 2017)

Indeed, in past years when the negative sentiment toward Russian international politics has significantly increased among foreign audiences, the Hermitage Foundations' main supporters and stakeholders remained very loyal to the museum (Sirakanian 2017). A new branch of the Hermitage Foundation in Finland was successfully established in 2016, and a new Hermitage satellite in Barcelona is planned to open in the future. This is evidence that the International Hermitage Network provides a robust, reliable and sustainable platform to further cultural diplomacy. As Sirakanian explained: "the main chairpersons and board of directors of foundations in different countries are powerful people abroad, so called 'decision-makers' and they can influence certain aspects in political climate," leading to improving official international relations (Sirakanian 2017).

The case of the Hermitage illuminates that museum franchising activities can significantly contribute to a national government's strategic efforts and agenda in cultural diplomacy. Exercised in such an authoritarian political regime as Russia, in which museums are still heavily dependent on the national government, the Hermitage network diplomacy offers an example that is particularly important. It exposes the growing capacity of museums to develop direct international connections with foreign stakeholders and constituencies, bypassing governmental control.

Conclusion

This chapter demonstrated how Krens's business model of museum franchising has been initiated and trialled by Guggenheim. It also documented how this model was gradually transformed into a new network diplomacy in the context of the Hermitage Museum. While the Guggenheim global expansion practices through franchising are currently in decline, the Hermitage International Network is rapidly growing. A comparison between the two cases – the Guggenheim and the Hermitage – reveals striking differences in terms of how two institutions approached the idea of museum franchising.

The Guggenheim's quite aggressive franchising experiments are very often associated with forces of American imperialism or neo-colonisation. The State Hermitage, however, appears to enjoy strong public support from local communities and does not attract such severe criticism. In the case of the Guggenheim, Krens's ambitious global plans and projects were primarily informed by corporate logic and the profit-seeking interests of involved stakeholders. Guggenheim tried to implant new branches, based on the results of feasibility studies that were conducted by participating cities, mainly to explore the economic potential of new satellites. In contrast, the Hermitage approach to franchising has been always focused on productive relationship building with local artists, communities and wealthy patrons.

Indeed, the Hermitage International Network also started out of economic necessity and was intended to generate funds in support of the museum outside Russia. But the director of the Hermitage recognised the importance of relationship building as the main priority. "Cultural relations, if you destroy them are very difficult to rebuild," Piotrovsky stressed. "We should use every opportunity to emphasize that supporting cultural connections now can have a positive effect in the long term" (Piotrovsky 2017a). In order to develop a strong global brand that invites satellites in different parts of the world, the Hermitage patiently pursued its institutional commitments by creating stronger relationships with international partners.

Neil MacGregor, former Director of the British Museum and an honourable member of the Hermitage Board of Trustees, described Piotrovsky as the "world's bravest champion of the Enlightenment idea that culture trumps politics [. . .] He has striven to keep the feel of a museum of the nineteenth century while dragging the Hermitage into the 21st and has succeeded spectacularly" (Hoyle 2014). Indeed, while experimenting with new business practices, the museum in Russia remained very loyal to its commitment and world-recognised reputation for highly artistic scholarship in its collections and exhibitions. The Hermitage brand is different in this sense from the Guggenheim brand, which is based on responsible populism logic.

"A museum is more like a temple than Disneyland or a computerized warehouse," Piotrovsky once remarked. "We try to show all that and instil it in society" through "our ambitious projects in Petersburg, in Kazan, in Yekaterinburg, in Amsterdam, in Omsk, in Venice, in Vladivostok, in Shanghai and in Moscow" (SHM 2017d). In one of his earlier interviews he also said: "the Hermitage is a powerful international corporation. It has many of the same rules as a corporation, but many different ones too. The main thing is that profit is not the criterion of success" (Kishkovsky 2009). This stands in opposition to Krens's philosophy of museum franchising that primarily rests on the "economies of scale via a global network."

When the first franchise museum opened its doors in Bilbao in 1997, Krens envisioned: "With a dazzling and popular art museum, our cities, can become tourist magnets, commercial hubs, and global players. It's a can't-miss investment" (Brenson 2004, 283).

The case of the Hermitage illustrates that the sustainability of museum franchises, which are now mushrooming throughout the world, draws on a museum's capacity to develop long-term and mutually beneficial relationships with hosting communities across cultural and political elites, as well as general publics. While the Hermitage franchising seems to be a departure from the original museum franchise idea developed by Guggenheim, both cases are based on building powerful museum brands. The State Hermitage and the Guggenheim were successful in building strong recognition, visibility and appreciation among their respected international constituencies.

In the case of the Guggenheim, though, local authorities and transnational corporations were keen to develop franchise partnerships in pursuit of their economic interests. But in the case of the Hermitage, the interests of involved stakeholders usually go beyond pure economics and are based on multiple goals ranging from political to cultural. The Director of the Development Department at the Hermitage explained that foreign stakeholders are attracted by the powerful global image and brand of the Hermitage as a world museum with rich and diverse collections. "In some cases, by developing links with the Hermitage Museum, potential international stakeholders are seeking pathways to establish stronger relationships within professional and political networks in which the museum is heavily involved" (Sirakanian 2017).

As the second part of the chapter revealed, the Hermitage's global reputation is powerful in engaging wealthy patrons, mobilising the Russian diaspora community, attracting local artists and curators and developing strong connections with local hosting communities through cultural exchanges. This precise difference is what makes the Hermitage International Network a global non-state player of cultural diplomacy. This potential has not yet been realised through the Guggenheim franchise. The case of enduring and productive Hermitage network diplomacy illustrates that museum franchising could be employed to serve the purposes of cultural diplomacy.

More importantly, this case demonstrates that museum franchises empower national museums from authoritarian regimes, such as Russia, to find new sources of support for meaningful international exchanges and connections that bypass governmental control and engage private funding. Furthermore, the Hermitage diplomacy offers a case that is particularly important. It exposes the growing capacity of museums to outperform their national governments in exercising productive cultural diplomacy that does not evoke negative sentiment and controversy.

In recent years, the Russian government has striven to boost its international image through multimillion-dollar public diplomacy campaigns, such as the Sochi Olympics 2014 and the FIFA World Cup 2018. However, in many cases these efforts were portrayed in the global media and academia as "old public diplomacy" or a "one-way flow of communication" (Pamment 2013) that lacks credibility and can be better understood as channels of Russian propaganda (Rawnsley 2015). The case of the Hermitage, though, clearly illustrates that authoritarian-based states, like Russia, can draw on the soft power of their non-state actors. Beyond the Russian government's attempts to exercise public diplomacy, there is a new type of actor emerging from within the national political climate, giving a birth to a new form of non-state cultural diplomacy. The State Hermitage Museum found ways to go global and attract audiences and constituencies from different countries without relying on the Russian government's support or patronage. Instead, the Russian government now relies on the Hermitage outposts abroad as sites for official diplomacy.

References

Abrams, Amah-Rose. 2017. Ex-Guggenheim Director Thomas Krens Thinks Abu Dhabi Project Should Be Scaled Back. *Art News*, 30 March.

Abu Dhabi Tourism & Culture Authority (ADT&CA). 2017. Museums. https://bit.ly/2itqE2V (accessed July 2017).

Azua, Jon. 2005. Guggenheim Bilbao: "Competitive" Strategies for the New Culture Economy Spaces. In *Learning from the Bilbao Guggenheim*, eds. Ana María Guasch and Joseba Zulaika, 77–100. Reno: University of Nevada.

Baigarova, Ksenya. 2014. Hermitage Receives $2 Million Birthday Present from American Collector. *Russia Beyond the Headlines*, 13 November.

Bernshausen, Sara. 2011. Interview by Natalia Grincheva.

Bradley, Kim. 1997. The Deal of the Century: Planning Process for Guggenheim Museum Bilbao, Spain. *Art in America* 85: 48–55.

Brenson, Michael. 2004. *Acts of Engagement: Writings on Art, Criticism, and Institutions, 1993–2002*. Rowman & Littlefield.

Celso, Fioravante. 2001. Booty and Soul. *Art Forum International* 39(6).

dal Col, Francesco and Kurt Forster. 1998. *Frank O. Gehry: The Complete Works.* New York, NY: Monacelli Press.

Decker, Darla. 2008. *Urban Development, Cultural Clusters: The Guggenheim Museum and Its Global Distribution Strategies*. New York University.

Deutsche Bank. 2007. Deutsche Bank Art. http://bit.ly/1KigrRf (accessed March 2015).

Deutsche Guggenheim. 1999. 1 + 1 = 3. www.deutsche-bank-kunst.com/guggenheim (accessed March 2015).

Digout, Amy. 2006. *Courting the West: Nicholas I, Cultural Diplomacy and the State Hermitage Museum in 1852*. Montreal: McGill University Press.

Dolan, David. 1999. Cultural Franchising, Imperialism and Globalisation: What's New? *International Journal of Heritage Studies* 5(1): 58–64.

Ellis, Adrian. 2007. A Francise Model for the Few – Very Few. *The Art Newspaper*, 1 October.

Elsheshtawy, Yasser. 2012. The Production of Culture: Abu Dhabi's Urban Strategies. In *Cultures and Globalization*, eds. Helmut K Anheier and Yudhishthir Raj Isar. Lonodn: Sage.

Esterow, Milton. 2001. From Slot Machines to the Sublime. *Art News* 100(11).

Fabelová, Karolína. 2010. Museums for Sale: The Louvre and Guggenheim in Abu Dhabi New Presence. *The Prague Journal of Central European Affairs* 12(2): 53–58.

Gall, Lothar, Buschen, Hans, Feldman, Gerald, Holtfrerich, Carl-Ludwig and Harold. James 1995. *The Deutsche Bank: 1870-1995*. London: Weindenfeld & Nicolson.

Gibson, Stuart. 2003. The Hermitage and Institutional Change: A Leap into the Twenty-first Century. *Museum International* 55(1): 20–26.

Goff, Patricia. 2017. The Museum as a Transnational Actor. *Arts and International Affairs* 2(1).

Grincheva, Natalia. 2010. Screening of the Hermitage Dwellers in Washington, D.C., Hermitage Museum Foundation, USA News Letter, September 2010. http://bit.ly/2v4GuXtRPDS (accessed November 2018).

Grincheva, Natalia. 2017. Sustainable Fundraising in the 21st Century: Behind the Scenes of the Global Guggenheim Success. In *Systems Thinking in Museums: Theory and Practice*, eds. Yuha Jung and Ann Love, 181–190. Rowman & Littlefield.

Guggenheim, Peggy. 1987. *Out of this Century: Confessions of an Art Addict*. Universe Publishing.

Guggenheim, Peggy. 1993. *Art of This Century: The Guggenheim Museum and Its Collection*. New York, NY: Solomon R. Guggenheim Foundation.

Guggenheim, Peggy. 2000a. Guggenheim Museum Bilbao. http://bit.ly/1B1evmf (accessed March 2015).

Guggenheim, Peggy. 2000b. Press Release, 27 September: Guggenheim Alliance with Gehry and Koolhaas. http://bit.ly/1NkMZZ7 (accessed March 2015).

Guggenheim, Peggy. 2002. Brazil: Body and Soul. http://bit.ly/1eD01Fq (accessed March 2015).

Guggenheim, Peggy. 2006. 30,000-Square-Meter Landmark to Establish UAE Capital as Global Cultural Destination. http://bit.ly/1MKBsmb (accessed March 2015).

Guggenheim, Peggy. 2013. Architecture. http://bit.ly/1akZsu2 (accessed March 2015).

Haacke, Hans. 2005. The Guggenheim Museum: A Business Plan. In *Learning from the Guggenheim Bilbao*, eds. Ana María Guasch and Joseba Zulaika, 113–123. Reno: Center for Basque Studies, University of Nevada.

Hansen, Liane and Flo Rogers. 2003. Las Vegas Closes Its Door. *Weekend Edition Sunday*, 18 May.

Harold, James. 2001. *The Deutsche Bank and the Nazi Economic War Against the Jews*. Cambridge, MA: Cambridge University Press.

Heilbrun, James. 2010. Managing a Museum's Collection. *The Journal of Arts Management, Law, and Society* 23(1): 69–76.

Hermitage Amsterdam (HA). 2017. Organization. www.hermitage.nl/en/organisatie/ (accessed November 2018).

Hermitage Museum Foundation, UK (HMF UK). 2017. Visiting Curators. http://bit.ly/2wvmVLu (accessed November 2018).

Hermitage Museum Foundation, USA (HMF USA). 2017. Art from America. http://bit.ly/2v5duib (accessed November 2018).

Hoyle, Beatrice. 2014. Hermitage Museum's Bridge Between Culture and Power. *The Australian*, 11 December.

Ilienko-Chung, Tataiana. 2014. White Russian Nostalgia for Their Ancestors' Homeland. *Global City NYC*. https://bit.ly/2BtshYG (accessed November 2018).

Kaufman, Jason. 2003. A Guggenheim for Brazil. *Art Newspaper*, 6.

Kaufman, Jason. 2004. Taiwan and Brazil Have Second Thoughts About Guggenheim. *Art Newspaper*, 14.

Kishkovsky, Sophia. 2009. Building a Greater Hermitage. *Art News*, 1 September.

Knöfel, Ulrike and von Dewitz, Ariane. 2008. Guggenheim Abu Dhabi Will Be "Pharaonic." *Spiegel*, 27 March.

Krauss, Rosalind. 1990. The Cultural Logic of the Late Capitalist Museum. *The MIT Press* 54(1): 3–17.

KunstHalle. 2015. Exhibitions and Programs. http://bit.ly/2uRX0gx (accessed March 2015).

Lawson-Johnston, Peter. 2014. *Growing Up Guggenheim: A Personal History of a Family Enterprise*. New York, NY: Open Road Media.

Lund, Ragnar and Stephen A. Greyser. 2015. *Corporate Sponsorship in Culture*. Boston, MA: Harvard Business School.

Mamaeva, Tatiana. 2017. Mikhail Piotrovsky: "Petersburg Citizens Were Not Asked About the Fate of St Isaac's Cathedral, It Is Insulting." *Real Time*, 23 October.

Martinez, Jill. 2001. *Financing a Global Guggenheim Museum*. University of South Carolina.

Marwick, Peat. 1998. *Impact of the Activities of the Fundacion del Museo Guggenheim Bilbao on the Basque Country*. Bilbao: Eustat - Euskal Estatistika Erakundea - Instituto Vasco de Estadística.

Mathur, Saloni. 2005. Social Thought and Commentary: Museums and Globalization. *Anthropological Quarterly* 78(3): 3697–3708.

Matveev, Vladimir. 2003. The Hermitage and Its Links with Regions of Russia. *Museum International* 55(1): 68–74.

Mediguren, Ibon. 2001. Boomtown Basque. *Art Newspaper*, 12.

The Ministry of Foreign Affairs of the Russian Federation (MFARF). 2016. Foreign Policy Concept of the Russian Federation (approved by President of the Russian Federation Vladimir Putin on November 30, 2016). https://bit.ly/2qb0l5Z (accessed May 2018).

Muschamp, Herbert. 2002. When Art Puts Down a Bet in a House of Games. *New York Times*, 14 April.

Newhouse, Victoria. 1998. *Towards a New Museum*. New York, NY: Monacelli Press.

Norman, Geraldine. 2005. *The Hermitage: The Biography of a Great Museum*. London: Jonathan Cape.

Ourossof, Nicolai. 2010. Building museums and a fresh Arab identity. *The New York Times,* 26 November.

Pamment, James. 2013. *New Public Diplomacy in the 21st Century: A Comparative Study of Policy and Practice*. London: Routledge.

Peterson, Kristen. 2008. Guggenheim-Hermitage Still in the Game. *Las Vegas Sun*, 23 October.

Piotrovsky, Mikhail. 2003. The Hermitage Through the Centuries. *Museum International* 217(55): 9–11.

Piotrovsky, Mikhail. 2017a. Art Above Politics. Hermitage Museum Foundation, USA. http://bit.ly/2fXwdty (accessed November 2018).

Piotrovsky, Mikhail. 2017b. President Vladimir Putin Presents the State Prize to Mikhail Piotrovsky, General Director of the State Hermitage. https://bit.ly/2SZa6B7 (accessed November 2018).

Plaza, Beatriz, Tironi, Manuel and Silke N. Haarich. 2009. Bilbao's Art Scene and the "Guggenheim Effect" Revisited. *European Planning Studies* 17(11): 1711–1729.

Prevots, Naima. 2001. *Dance for Export: Cultural Diplomacy and the Cold War*. Middletown, OH: Wesleyan University Press.

Radzevicius, Vytas. 2011. Guggenheim Museum Initiative in Vilnius to Be Taken Over by the Finns. *The Lithuania Tribune*, 7 February.

Rauen, Marjorie. 2001. Reflections on the Space of Flows: The Guggenheim Museum Bilbao. *The Journal of Arts Management, Law, and Society* 30(4): 283–300.

Rawnsley, Gary D. 2015. To Know Us Is to Love Us: Public Diplomacy and International Broadcasting in Contemporary Russia and China. *Politics* 35(3–4): 273–286.

Wise, Michael. 2014. Rethinking the Guggenheim Helsinki. *Art News.* 25 September.

Ruiz, Cristina. 2017. Guggenheim Abu Dhabi Should Be Postponed or Downsized, Says the Man Who Launched the Project. *Art Newspaper*, 26 March.

Russian Cultural Centre (RCC). 2017. About Us. http://rccusa.org/ (accessed November 2018).

Rymer, Thomas. 2000. Hermitage Meets Its Modern Match. *The St. Petersburg Times,* 23 June.

Siegal, Nina. 2016. Guggenheim Helsinki Museum Plans Are Rejected. *New York Times*, 30 November.

Sorkin, Michael. 2005. Brand Aid or the Lexus and the Guggenheim (Further Tales of the Notorious B.I.G.ness). In *Commodifi cation and Spectacle in Architecture,* ed. William Saunders, 22–33. Minneapolis, MN: University of Minnesota Press.

Sirakanian, Katia. 2017. Interview by Natalia Grincheva.

Smale, Alison. 2009. A Russian Affair with Amsterdam. *New York Times*, 26 June.

Sorkin, Michael. 2005. Brand Aid or the Lexus and the Guggenheim (Further Tales of the Notorious B.I.G.ness). In *Commodifi cation and Spectacle in Architecture.*

State Hermitage Museum (SHM). 2005. Hermitage Kazan. http://bit.ly/2fZybJV (accessed November 2018).

State Hermitage Museum (SHM). 2007. The Hermitage–Italy Centre. http://bit.ly/2wiFeUt (accessed November 2018).

State Hermitage Museum (SHM). 2010–2014. Annual Report 2010–2014. http://bit.ly/2x4yLdB (accessed November 2018).

State Hermitage Museum (SHM). 2017a. Hermitage Friends' Organizations outside Russia. http://bit.ly/2gbrsLA (accessed November 2018).

State Hermitage Museum (SHM). 2017b. Gala Banquet in the Winter Palace. http://bit.ly/2gbrsLA (accessed November 2018).

State Hermitage Museum (SHM). 2017c. Dutch Friends of the Hermitage. http://bit.ly/2wvkskn (accessed November 2018).

State Hermitage Museum (SHM). 2017d. President Vladimir Putin Presents the State Prize to Mikhail Piotrovsky, General Director of the State Hermitage. https://bit.ly/2HCwm0N (accessed November 2018).

Statista. 2018. Annual Evolution of the Number of Visitors to the Guggenheim Museum Bilbao (Spain) from 2010 to 2017. https://bit.ly/2GsZcSD (accessed November 2018).

Sylvester, Christine. 2009. *Art/Museums: International Relations Where We Least Expect It*. London: Paradigm Publishers.

Trilupaityte, Skaidra. 2009. Guggenheim's Global Travel and the Appropriation of a National Avant-Garde for Cultural Planning in Vilnius. *International Journal of Cultural Policy* 15(1): 123–138.

Tromp, Jan. 2009. The Inspiration Behind the Hermitage Amsterdam. In *Amstelhof Hermitage Amsterdam: From Nursing Home to Museum*, eds. Nelleke Noordervliet, Carina van Aartsen, Jan Tromp and Hans Ibelings, 194–219. Amsterdam: Hermitage Amsterdam.

Varoli, John. 2000. Guggenheim and Hermitage Forge an Alliance. *Art Newspaper*, 105.

Vivant, Elsa. 2011. Who Brands Whom? The Role of Local Authorities in the Branching of Art Museums. *Town Planning Review* 82(1): 99–115.

Vogel, Carol. 2003. Guggenheim Grows: The Next Stop Is Rio. *The New York Times*, 1 May.

Vogel, Carol. 2012. Guggenheim Project Challenges "Western-Centric View." *Art & Design*, 11 April.

Wainwright, Oliver. 2014. Helsinki v Guggenheim: The Backlash Against the Global Megabrand Is on. *Guardian*, 11 September.

Werner, Paul. 2005. *Museum Inc: Inside the Global Art World*. Chicago, IL: Prickly Paradigm Press.

Wilson, Jeanne L. 2015. Russia and China Respond to Soft Power: Interpretation and Readaptation of a Western Construct. *Politics* 35(3–4): 287–300, 294.

Wise, Michael. 2014. An Open Design Competition for a New Museum in the Finnish Capital Reflects a Change in the Foundation's Global Strategy. *Art News*, 25 August.

Wu, Chin-Tao. 2002. *Privatising Culture. Corporate Art Intervention Since the 1980s*. London: Verso.

Wyma, Chloe. 2014. 1% Museum: The Guggenheim Goes Global. *Dissent*, 15 August.

Zulaika, Joseba. 2001. Krens's Taj Mahal: The Guggenheim's Global Love Museum. *Discourse* 23(1): 100–118.

Conclusion

Museum diplomacy in the neo-liberal age

This book documents the development of new forms, channels of operations and sources of support for contemporary museum diplomacy. It demonstrates that, in the twenty-first century, museums gain access to international resources and establish connections with international audiences and constituencies in ways that no longer require support or patronage from their respective governments. New conditions of neo-liberal globalisation transform museums from institutions exclusively dependent on national public funding into more multi-faceted actors in the global economic sector of culture. These transformations manifest in increasing convergence between museums as public intuitions with cultural and social missions and for-profit corporations with distinct economic agendas and goals. These transformations affect museum diplomacy, offering new approaches and ways they can be conceived, designed and implemented.

Diplomacy at the edge of convergence between museums and transnational corporations

International interests and activities of market-oriented corporations and non-profit public institutions, such as museums, progressively converge (Rectanus 2002). Museums increasingly adopt corporate practices, while corporations assume museums' functions in mediating cultural artefacts and experiences (Rectanus 2002, 175). What previously remained unclear, though, is how this convergence impacts contemporary practices of cultural diplomacy and if it enables non-state forms of museum diplomacy.

Diplomacy scholarship argued that transnational corporations are the most powerful among non-state actors (Ataman 2003; Spiro 2013). Economic power allows corporations to leverage their interests by directly bargaining with national governments for favourable policies, either through promises of new investment or threats of withdrawal (Nye 2004, 156). More importantly, "modern corporations seek to develop their active participation in society, adding new dimensions to their traditionally perceived role of generating wealth, employment, and quality products or services" (Ordeix-Rigo and Duarte 2009, 557). To make their brands more appealing in the eyes of global consumers, corporations invest considerable resources in supporting cultural and social causes, facilitating "bidirectional processes to engage publics" (Grunig et al. 2002).

A good illustration is the Google Cultural Institute, founded in 2011 as a "not-for-profit initiative that partners with cultural organisations to bring the world's cultural heritage online" (Google 2015). This institute has been working closely with museums around the world, providing free tools, expertise and resources to digitise global cultural heritage and make museums "more widely accessible to a global audience" (Google 2015). The investment in this multimillion-dollar initiative is not purely philanthropic in nature. It intends to develop and diversify the global market of Google customers and bypass political boundaries.

For example, while Google suffers from the Great Firewall policies in China, the Google Cultural Institute hosts 31 online collections of major Chinese museums. It even includes artworks from the Palace Museum in Beijing, one of the most significant icons of national culture. The museum was designated in 1961 by the State Council as one of China's foremost-protected cultural heritage sites (Li et al. 2014). Such global exposure of Chinese museums and collections is welcomed by the national government, despite its strict protectionist media policies. China strives to catch up with the Western world in developing its cultural infrastructure and projecting its soft power (Zhang 2016). The Google Cultural Institute offers a solution, temporally free and seemingly safe.

The convergence between corporations and museums on the global stage goes in two directions. It is not only global corporations, such as Google, that increasingly get involved in international cultural activities that impact museums and world audiences. As this book demonstrates, museums progressively adopt business modes of operation employed by transnational corporations that allow them to go global to reach new audiences and implement ambitious international projects. Global corporatisation and museum franchising, pioneered by the Guggenheim, have provided new ways for museum operations in the global cultural economy. Thomas Krens boldly experimented with both practices to "make the Guggenheim an international corporation interested in questions of growth and expansion, as well as stimulating business in the visual arts" (Guasch and Zulaika 2005, 17).

Krens was condemned for implementing business models, including an "international network of branch museums, ties to corporations, [. . .] and exhibitions featuring luxury consumer products" (Fraser 2006, 56). However, these models initiated global museum trends that have a strong value beyond economics. This book offered two case studies from Russia and China that evidenced the employment of global corporatisation and museum franchising for museum expansion with strong implications for contemporary cultural diplomacy.

First, the K11 Art Mall example illustrated how powerful private actors in China's rapidly growing economy employ global corporatisation to support and promote contemporary national art while making it present and visible on the world stage. This arts commerce business model provided a convincing example of the culmination in the processes of convergence between a contemporary museum and a corporation. More importantly, it demonstrated that such a hybrid between a museum and for-profit business is capable of exercising cultural diplomacy on the world stage, projecting China's soft power.

Second, the International Network of Foundations of the State Hermitage Museum demonstrated the evolution of museum franchising from a global brand development strategy into a new avenue of cultural diplomacy. Numerous Hermitage Foundations and emerging branches in North America, Europe and Asia have built something more than just a franchise network, allowing the museum to secure economic support from international sources. They created opportunities for genuine cultural exchanges among artists, curators and communities that ultimately shaped new channels of cultural diplomacy, directly contributing to Russia's foreign policy agenda.

These new practices in cultural diplomacy exercised by museums beyond the Western world of developed countries are the result of global mutations of museums that nevertheless remain non-profit enterprises with important cultural missions. "Museums are not earning money for their shareholders, but rather to [. . .] conserve and exhibit art and to educate the public about it" (Goff 2017).

While the governance of the Solomon R. Guggenheim Foundation envisioned the museum in New York as becoming "the parent corporation" of franchise branches across the globe (Lawson-Johnston 2014), it remains a non-profit organisation with a tax-exempt charitable status. The Guggenheim benefits from its 501(c)(3) privileges, outlined in the U.S. Internal Revenue Service (IRS), which exempt the museum from having to pay taxes on its activities. Additionally, the museum receives financial support from a wide variety of corporate donors whose donations are also tax deductible.

Arguably, corporate models of global expansion developed under Krens offered a more sustainable and enduring economic platform to pursue the institutional mission of supporting and promoting contemporary arts. The analysis of the Guggenheim's IRS 990 tax reports from 2001–2012, for example, revealed that over several years the museum suffered a deficit in its operational budget, despite multimillion-dollar corporate pledges and self-earned revenue. This budget deficit proves that the Guggenheim's international programs are not exclusive to activities that only aim to generate economic capital. The growing appetite of the museum to engage global audiences and extend its recognition and visibility in different parts of the world comes at a price.

The book exposes, however, that the Guggenheim's international engagements, either through global corporatisation or museum franchises, have no intention of complementing the cultural diplomacy of the U.S.A. The museum, both under and post-Krens, has been more concerned about its own global brand development than creating long-term bridges of cross-cultural interactions with a distinct contribution to the U.S. foreign policy agenda. As Christine McLaren (2011), Canadian journalist and Guggenheim resident writer, once asked rhetorically: "Who needs to rule the American dream when you can rule the world?" Celebrating its own global mission and identity, the Guggenheim does not intend to act on behalf of the U.S. government as an actor of cultural diplomacy.

Its activities on the world stage, however, promote values of liberal democracy and free market forces, pushing toward neo-liberal globalisation. As the book demonstrates, these forces gave rise to museums beyond Western economies. These museums stand out on the world stage as projections of their own soft power, while acting as non-state players in cultural diplomacy.

Museum diplomacy as soft power of non-state actors

The director of the Hermitage once remarked, "art is more important than money. But money is not unimportant" (Tromp 2009, 202). In the twenty-first century, global corporatisation and museum franchising have given a museum agency reliable and sustainable tools to generate economic capital and implement international programming beyond national borders. Most importantly, this support does not come from national governments and is not closely tied to the strategic geopolitical agenda of nation states. These new practices of global expansion serve to liberate museums from a need to seek public funding from national budgets that always comes at a political cost. Instead, museums can employ the corporate models to pursue their own cultural missions in the global arena, at the same time indirectly contributing to cultural diplomacy of their respective countries.

Acting autonomously from government patronage, museums become non-state actors of cultural diplomacy, not through any official status but rather through their institutional legitimacy: expertise and credibility. The book presents case studies that illustrate how museums from different cultural contexts and political regimes build their global reputations by projecting strong expertise and credibility. Both the K11 Art Foundation and the International Network of Hermitage Foundations present compelling examples of museum brands that earn their diplomatic legitimacy while finding ways to implement their international programs through bypassing direct government control.

While the activities of K11 raise controversy among national art critics, who question the commercial model of art shopping malls, its partnerships with world-recognised museums around the world are growing. Numerous international artistic and curatorial exchanges and exhibitions in collaboration with famous institutions of contemporary arts – such as MoMA PS1 and New Museum in New York, the Institute of Contemporary Arts in London, Centre Pompidou and Palais de Tokyo in Paris – prove that K11 is gaining recognition in the global arts community. Not only does K11 systematically nurture its expertise through highly prestigious international arts engagements at Venice Biennale or Art Basel – it also builds trustworthy relationships with international communities of artists and institutions through cultural exchanges, while acting outside the Chinese government agenda in official cultural diplomacy.

Aiming to project the soft power of China, K11 offers alternative avenues of non-state diplomacy and works more productively than the national government in striving to rebrand the country in the international arena. Likewise, the credibility of the International Network of Hermitage Foundations and its international cultural exchanges is indisputable. It is undeniable that the Hermitage Museum is a state-sponsored actor, keeping strong ties with the Russian government. However, its network of international foundations mobilises foreign civil society and engages wealthy stakeholders from abroad, thus offering a different avenue of cultural diplomacy. This diplomacy is not commissioned, initiated or controlled by the Russian government and rests on the Hermitage's world-recognised expertise in museum scholarship. The credibility of the network of foundations and branches, and the museum's expertise to lead large-scale international projects, attracts substantial international resources to implement non-state museum diplomacy.

In both cases, museums are capable of generating soft power on behalf of their nation states, precisely because they act autonomously from their respective governments on the global stage. The diplomacy of K11 and the Hermitage Museum is self-initiated and conceived as a distinct cultural mission that aspires to advance national interests rather than the individual interests of involved stakeholders. Unlike Krens, Cheng and Piotrovsky have prioritised nurturing long-term international cultural relations with foreign audiences and institutions. These cultural exchanges do more than strengthen the sustainability of their international engagements with audiences and museums abroad. They are at the heart of a cultural diplomacy that works more efficiently than government-funded efforts in cultural promotions and national branding.

The Guggenheim's brand has also gained a strong international recognition, especially among local authorities and transnational corporations seeking to enhance their own brands on the world stage. However, in comparison to the soft power of the Hermitage and K11, which intentionally pursue the foreign policy objectives of their states, the Guggenheim's global attraction power takes a different form. Museum scholar Mark W. Rectanus (2002) has argued that the social power of contemporary museums to engage audiences and win global attention is not measured any longer through "pedagogy, educational power and excellence of artistic scholarship" (12). Instead, he defined the social power of museums in terms of "their public visibility, market success, and media reception," which can be accomplished "from a basis of economic capital (investments and sponsorships), as well as cultural capital (collections and exhibitions)" (Rectanus 2002, 12).

This formula has a lot of similarities with the Krensian economics of museum success, which rests on an institution's ability to effectively employ museum assets, "great collections, great architecture," to produce income through "economies of scale via a global network." The Guggenheim's economic capital, either generated through self-earned revenue or built through strategic partnerships with transnational corporations, not only ensures the museum's financial sustainability but also, more importantly, translates this economic capital further into the social power of the Guggenheim to attract public attention on a global scale.

The public attention, though, does not necessarily come with positive sentiments only. Cultural critics accuse Guggenheim of being a neo-liberal institution, "increasingly dependent on corporate gifts rather than public funding; that privileges traveling exhibitions over permanent collections, aspirational leisure over education, risk and innovation over cultural preservation" (Wyma 2014). However, in the age of growing neo-liberalism, as some scholars would argue, an institutional reputation primarily draws on organisational efficiency to attract larger audiences (Rodden 2006). Reputation is a new measure of social value, assessed though the ability of an organisation to act as a catalyst for flows of public attention and engagements (Arvidsson and Peitersen 2009).

The Guggenheim enjoys a high international visibility by mobilising international publics, through either its crowd-pleasing cultural offerings or bold McDonaldised interventions into local communities. Its brand's value is growing, especially appealing to transnational corporations or city authorities seek to capitalise on the museum's social power to attract large audiences to advance their own economic goals. The Guggenheim is a product of U.S. national culture, where a free market ideology dominates politics. However, global corporatisation and museum franchising piloted by Guggenheim are transformed from purely economic models to political projects once they travel beyond the borders of more democratic countries.

Global corporatisation and museum franchising as cultural diplomacy

Museums around the world gain more and more economic power by employing corporate models that facilitate their integration in the global cultural economy. At the same time, museums have always been political institutions (Gray 2015). Historically, museums developed from civilising tools to fulfil "the task of the cultural governance of the populace" (Bennett 1995, 21) into a means of constructing cultural communities (Anderson 2006). The international agenda of contemporary museology urges these institutions to be responsible social actors, "networked civil society institutions with soft power" (Lord and Blankenberg 2015, 19). Museums cannot escape their political dimension, whether they are heavily dependent on public funding, like the State Hermitage Museum, or are economically self-sufficient, like K11 Art Mall.

This book illuminates that global corporatisation and museum franchising can enhance the economic sustainability of museums, offering new sources of funding for their international programs. However, the examples of both K11 and the Hermitage illustrate that the Guggenheim's global expansion model has stronger political implications when adopted within more authoritarian political regime. Both Russian and Chinese examples of museum diplomacy demonstrate that economic models of global expansion do not necessarily change the political arrangements of the national environments in which museums coexist with their audiences, constituencies and governments.

In China, cultural politics and government incentives gave rise to thousands of new public and private museums that are growing in the country with the pace of development of the "China's high-speed railway network" (Gaskin 2014). The urgency to develop the cultural infrastructure to project a more culturally appealing image on the world stage has triggered a boom in the museum industry. In many cases, new museums in China arise from exclusively private sources of new generation of Chinese philanthropists. Yet they still have a very distinct political task. These museums serve the state to boost the cultural image of China in the international arena.

K11, as an apotheosis of the global corporatisation model employed by Chinese museums, is especially illustrative of the political agenda implemented on behalf of corporate actors. While privately funded, K11's global ambitions and programs offer a new platform for cultural exchanges between China and the Western world, facilitating non-state cultural diplomacy that thrives outside of the official government channels. But the political censorship of China's authoritarian regime ensures that K11's cultural activities on the global stage avoid raising politically sensitive issues that could compromise the government's image. As a result, global corporatisation, as a model, provides a new economic platform to exercise national politics and wield soft power.

In Russia, the State Hermitage Museum is one of the most important political actors among national cultural institutions. It has cultivated close ties with the government across generations, regardless of political forces in power, from imperial Russia through the communist era to the Russian Federation under Vladimir Putin. While enjoying its privileged status and special patronage from the Russian government, the Hermitage found ways to go global by securing new sources of support from the international community. Its unique chain of foundations and museum branches across continents generates economic revenue, not only to sustain itself and to host numerous Hermitage exhibitions, programs and community engagement events but also to help the museum in Saint Petersburg. More importantly, it paves the way for non-state cultural diplomacy beyond the control of the Russian government that, in contrast to national efforts, prioritises long-term cultural relations and mutually beneficial outcomes.

While keeping close connections with the government, the Hermitage is also eager to share its outposts in different countries as venues for negotiations and meetings of political elites and official channels of cultural diplomacy. The Russian government utilises these new "islands" of celebration of Russian culture, legacy and heritage abroad as important political spaces to communicate with international counterparts. Furthermore, while there is not a strong political censorship system as in China, the Hermitage has to navigate a national system of political regulations that sets limitations on freedom of artistic expression.

For example, in 2014, when the Hermitage hosted Manifesta 10, the travelling European biennial, it was challenged by new laws constraining LGBT rights in Russia and, more importantly, by a complex political situation in Crimea. Against all odds, the exhibition took place at Winter Palace, the Hermitage main building. However, Piotrovsky revealed:

> We need to do everything within the limits of the law and not be showing propaganda. [Russian law prohibits the display of "gay propaganda."] We addressed a lot of issues with this exhibition: the "gay" question, Ukraine. . . . But not in a way that was a provocation.
>
> (Groskop 2014)

While both cases, the Hermitage and K11, demonstrate that museums in more authoritarian regimes are a subject of political control, they also illuminate significant transformations of cultural diplomacy in the twenty-first century.

By providing economic support for museums' international activities, global corporatisation and museum franchising considerably change the power dynamics in design, focus and form of cultural diplomacy activities. Employing models of global expansion, museums gain power to initiate, plan and structure their international exhibitions and exchange projects. Furthermore, taking initiative into their hands, museums acquire a greater freedom to choose where to go, what to exhibit and with which communities to engage. This choice is not guided any longer by geopolitical necessities dictated by national governments.

Nevertheless, global corporatisation and museum franchising are not a panacea that completely liberates museums in their institutional choices in international initiatives. As the case of the Guggenheim demonstrates, global expansion practices, at the expense of powerful corporate patrons, notably shape and influence museums' international activities and even damage credibility and reputation among dedicated artistic communities.

Museums should try to keep a healthy balance between politics and economics of global engagements. If such a compromise is achieved, global corporatisation and museum franchising can help museums grow their global brands, attract international investment and build cross-cultural bridges of mutual trust and understanding. Capitalising on private and corporate resources, as well as their own expertise and global recognition, museums can become vital players of cultural diplomacy that progressively transcend traditional channels of government initiatives.

The main contribution of this book is a comparative analysis of several case studies that explicitly demonstrates a shift in museums' international activities from a political endeavour to a more autonomous pursuit of institutional missions. These are driven by both economic interests and cultural ambitions on the global scale. This book has started a conversation about the implications of new forms of international museum engagements for the field of cultural diplomacy. But it also intends to encourage further dialogue and investigation of the development of new trends in museum diplomacy.

Beyond such practices as museum franchising and global corporatisation, museums have already trialled a variety of new management models that aim to enhance their economic standing, social outreach and cultural influence at home and abroad. They include, but are not limited to, collaborations with creative communities of cultural and digital entrepreneurs and establishing international labs or hubs for innovative scientific research.

They also include digital experimentation – ranging from viral social media campaigns to virtual and augmented reality projects – that take the audience beyond the limits of the physical world. These practices are worth further exploration, especially in relation to their implications for contemporary diplomacy.

Museum diplomacy is dynamic. It reflects social, cultural and political changes taking place throughout the world. This book has documented how museum franchising and global corporatisation have challenged and innovated museum diplomacy in the era of neo-liberal globalisation. This research is intended to inspire further exploration of new trends in cultural diplomacy across museums and their cultural and political geographies.

References

Anderson, Benedict. 2006. *Imagined Communities*. London: Verso.

Arvidsson, Adam and Nicolai Peitersen. 2009. *The Ethical Economy*. New York, NY: Columbia University Press.

Ataman, Muhittin. 2003. The Impact of Non-State Actors on World Politics: A Challenge to Nation-States. *Alternatives* 2(1): 42–66.

Bennett, Tony. 1995. *The Birth of the Museum: History, Theory, Politics*. London: Routledge.

Fraser, Andrea. 2006. Isn't This a Wonderful Place? (A Tour of a Tour of the Guggenheim Bilbao). In *Museum Frictions,* eds. Ivan Karp and Corinne Kratz, 135–160. Durham, NC: Duke University Press.

Gaskin, Sam. 2014. China's Aggressive Museum Growth Brings Architectural Wonders. *CNN*, 30 April.

Goff, Patricia. 2017. The Museum as a Transnational Actor. *Arts and International Affairs* 2(1).

Google. 2015. Google Cultural Institute. www.google.com/culturalinstitute (accessed March 2015).

Gray, Clive. 2015. *The Politics of Museums*. London: Palgrave Macmillan.

Groskop, Viv. 2014. Mikhail Piotrovsky: "Culture Is Always above Politics." *The Guardian*, 7 February.

Grunig, James, Dozier, David and D. Dossier. 2002. *Excellent Public Relations and Effective Organizations: A Study of Communication Management in Three Countries*. Mahwah, NJ: Lawrence Erlbaum.

Guasch, Anna Maria and Joseba Zulaika. 2005. *Learning from the Guggenheim Bilbao*. Reno: Center for Basque Studies, University of Nevada.

Lawson-Johnston, Peter. 2014. *Growing Up Guggenheim: A Personal History of a Family Enterprise*. New York, NY: Open Road Media.

Lord, Gail and Ngaire Blankenberg. 2015. *Museums, Cities and Soft Power.* Washington, DC: American Association of Museums.

Li, Jian, He, Li, Sung, Hou-mei and Ma Shengnan. 2014. *Forbidden City: Imperial Treasures from the Palace Museum, Beijing*. Virginia Museum of Fine Arts.

McLaren, Christine. 2011. New York City, the Capital of Capitals: Who Needs to Rule the American Dream When You Can Rule the World? *Guggenheim*. http://bit.ly/1GZp4uw (accessed November 2018).

Nye, Joseph. 2004. Multinational Corporations in World Politics. *Foreign Affairs* 53(1): 153–175.

Ordeix-Rigo, Enric and João Duarte. 2009. From Public Diplomacy to Corporate Diplomacy: Increasing Corporation's Legitimacy and Influence. *American Behavioral Scientist* 53(4): 549–564.

Rectanus, Mark. 2002. *Culture Incorporated: Museums, Artists and Corporate Sponsorship*. Minneapolis, MN: University of Minnesota.

Rodden, John. 2006. Reputation and Its Vicissitudes. *Society* 43(3): 75–80.

Spiro, Peter. 2013. Constraining Global Corporate Power: A Short Introduction. *Vanderbilt Journal of Transnational Law* 46: 1101–1118.

Tromp, Jan. 2009. The Inspiration Behind the Hermitage Amsterdam. In *Amstelhof Hermitage Amsterdam: From Nursing Home to Museum*, eds. Nelleke Noordervliet, Carina van Aartsen, Jan Tromp and Hans Ibelings, 194–219. Amsterdam: Hermitage Amsterdam.

Wyma, Chloe. 2014. 1% Museum: The Guggenheim Goes Global. *Dissent*, 15 August.

Zhang, Guozuo. 2016. *Research Outline for China's Cultural Soft Power*. Singapore: Springer.

Index

For Product Safety Concerns and Information please contact our EU representative GPSR@taylorandfrancis.com
Taylor & Francis Verlag GmbH, Kaufingerstraße 24, 80331 München, Germany

www.ingramcontent.com/pod-product-compliance
Lightning Source LLC
LaVergne TN
LVHW020639100826
845148LV00012B/2253

9780367787943